So a Bunch of Us Sat Down to Write...

THE HADDAM WRITERS GROUP

ISBN: 978-1-9791-8190-7

Contact us at HaddamWritersGroup@gmail.com

Available from Amazon.com and other book stores

Cover and interior design: Michael J. Gordon
Cover photos: James E. McKie, Jr.
Production: Robert Golden

For all who love to write,
and all who love to read.

Table of Contents

Preface

So far, the Brainerd Memorial Library staff has not asked us to leave. Not one of them has even said "Shush!" or requested that we move our meetings out into the parking lot. This is mildly surprising, since when we assemble in its building every week to review each others' works in progress, the resulting critiques, suggestions, and humor can often become quite animated—and loud.

The nine writers in our group come from diverse backgrounds: teacher, minister, antiques dealer, journalists, adjunct college professors, and scientists. Every one is passionate about writing.

In this book, you will encounter fiction and memoir, humor and sadness, a diversity of voices, styles, experiences, and outlooks. Each of us has learned something from the others' writings. Perhaps you might as well.

Feel free to peruse these short works in any order you like, from front to back, back to front, or hopping, skipping, and jumping around. Any way that entices or intrigues is fine. However you do it, we trust that you will enjoy reading what resulted when "A Bunch of Us Sat Down to Write."

The Haddam Writers Group

ISABELLE DOUGLAS SEGGERMAN

Red Ladybug

I am the voyeur who has watched a group of artists for the past few years. I was born with an abiding interest in human nature. I have observed the victors and the vanquished, the power of one, and the folly of many. Join me in this kaleidoscope, a tale of camaraderie and betrayal.

These artists joined together willingly, and they became what I shall refer to as "My Circle of Seven." Their common bond was the belief that by painting together they could achieve more artistically as well as commercially. So, besides their paint brushes and easels, each came fully equipped with a multitude of life experience to share—strong talent, pride, prejudice, and personal sensitivities.

It would be one of these elements that led to a crisis within the circle. It was only a matter of time—in this case, three years for the Waterloo and its potential for leaving the scars of battle upon each soul.

They met while taking a self-portrait class at the Lyme Academy. These highly skilled and talented artists (some professional and some close to) painted together once a week for two and a half months, studying under the remarkable Sabine. Some in the original group of seventeen came to learn a new discipline, that of portraiture; others came to learn new techniques. A few desired to work in a group situation for additional inspiration and motivation. One or two joined because they simply liked being students.

After a session, the group critiqued each other's painting,

generally quite gently. Sabine had a knack that was contagious. Her talent for pointing out the positive and best in each one's work inspired the entire group.

She once gave the class a fifteen minute exercise. They were to paint a self-portrait during that brief time. The purpose was to loosen the students' hands and brush strokes without leaving time for self-criticism or reworking the paintings. It was an exercise in spontaneous composition.

I observed with bated breath as Sabine began to critique a work that to me looked like a portrait of an inedible, overripe, bruised peach. Perhaps, the painter's grandmother? Yet, she found the beauty and strength on this canvas.

Her comment, "You have captured the blush of youth as well as an affinity for the aging process in this painting."

So, it was no surprise to me that her encouragement and inspiration lead a group of seven artists to continue painting together long after the course had been completed.

They found a circa 1900 brick building in a nearby village to use. It had once been the town's garage. Because of the brownfield left behind, it was too toxic for full-time use, but small groups could meet there occasionally without fear of chemical demise. The rent was right: FREE.

Their format was simple: Show up each week (unless something pressing like a trip to Italy, a sick spouse or a Girl Scout Retreat kept one away.) Subject matter could be whatever one chose. Some had tired of looking at themselves and chose to return to still-lives and landscapes. Others varied their subject matter weekly.

One excelled at restaurant scenes, painting tables absurdly over laden with lobsters, figs, melons, berries, and bread. Although I do not need much sustenance as I observe from my perch, my stomach always rumbled and my appetite increased when I viewed his work.

For three years, I watched the Seven as their painting developed and their skills increased. Having observed the living for so long, I believe that nothing is ever actually unique, so I find myself comparing this group's work to past masters.

Robin's renderings had the humor of a Charles Dana Gibson cartoon combined with the realism and technical skill of Norman Rockwell, while Angelique painted in a descriptive, touching, and spiritual style similar to Leonardo Da Vinci. Lulu approached her plein air painting in a scientific manner. If one of the stone walls she depicted had moss growing on it, by heaven it was the correct species and growing season for that bryophyte.

Georgianna was the group's Barbizon master. She was well traveled, and had an affinity for the French and Italian terrains as well as artistic talent—that is, provided she didn't go off into the clouds too much. Rosalie, on the other hand, was the least technically proficient. She painted in the 17th century, Flemish genre style. Her scenes depicted the everyday events, the joy and pathos of the commonplace, and the common man to which her viewers could relate.

Melissa contributed youth and humor to the Seven. While extremely accurate in her painting, she had a lyrical quality in each piece she presented. Her style reminded me of the Reynolds Beal circus series. It was light-hearted and joyful, while retaining an acute observation of human nature.

The Vermeer of the Seven was Eleanor, hands down. She painted with the accurate precision of the Dutch master. Her palette was cool. The colors she chose tended to be ice blues, soft slates, stark whites, charcoals and blacks.

Watching the Sevens' critiques of each other's work was a fairly straightforward observation. I think Sabine's tactful remarks remained in each one's mind, so the voice and opinion of each artist remained quite gentle, occasionally amusing, and generally accurate as they discussed the others' weekly production.

Once, Lulu painted a field of grain. Georgianna and Robin, deadpanning, wanted to know if the grain was gluten free.

Eleanor immediately took issue (one of her favorite phrases). She said that it was cruel to criticize the fact that many people had bad reactions to gluten and that it could do great harm to those with this type of food allergy.

After Eleanor's dampening comment, their attention turned to one of Georgianna's Barbizon landscapes. The others teased her mercilessly about the sky she had painted over three quarters of her canvas.

"Hey, don't forests have trees?" piped Angelique.

"Is this a skyscape or a landscape?" interjected Rosalie.

Georgianna was not amused by these comments, to say the least, but fortunately was sure enough of herself to take what she felt were irreverent and misguided critiques, and come up with a good retort.

"May lightning strike you all down from my sky, and preserve the trees which I have chosen not to paint!"

Then she burst out laughing.

Every once and awhile during the warm months, a few of the members would meet for a late lunch at a local dive on the Connecticut River.

Eleanor never participated in these spontaneous outings. She had an obsession about getting home to give her trained Rhesus monkey his peanuts at a specific time.

It was during the fall of the year 2014 that the innocent ladybug entered the circle and destroyed it. She appeared on the scene quietly and gently, as most of these little ladies do—or so I assumed. This is what I observed.

The group was, as always, good naturedly commenting on each other's productions. This day their concentrations were centered on Eleanor's latest academic interior. Rosalie, with her usual outspokenness and facetious sense of humor, blurted out, "What about adding a red ladybug to this chilly scene? It's atypical to the renderings of 17th century Dutch rooms, but perhaps a little twist, a surprise element, or just a dash of color might add intrigue to this scene." Robin and Lulu concurred.

As soon as the session ended, Eleanor picked up her easel, tossed her brushes into her paint box and departed. It was a wee bit abrupt. I think she had had quite enough of the Circle's colorful imaginations, at least for today. Despite most artists having a tolerance for each other's quirks, her departure, unfortunately, signified more—as Rosalie was to discover the following week.

The phone rang at nine a.m. on the group's next meeting day. Rosalie answered in a sleepy voice. Although she had been up since six to let the dogs out, she had not finished her second cup of coffee when the call came. It was Eleanor, to announce that she was resigning from the group.

"Rosalie, don't even try to change my mind as you have done in the past," spat out Eleanor.

"I have no intention of changing your mind. You gave this group your best shot. Perhaps, that is all you have to give," came the reply. "However, I would like to know, so that I could understand better, what has prompted this resignation?"

The response was short, swift and very much to Eleanor's point of view. "None of you are up to my intellectual or technical level. None of you have supported me or understood what I depict on canvas. You just nitpick about shades of color and my tonal palette. You offer me no support. All of you had the audacity to take one of the highest and purest forms of Dutch painting and attempt to bastardize it by suggesting to add a bug...a bug! And a warrior red colored one at that!'

With the call completed, Rosalie leaned over and patted her two dogs, finding solace in their smiles and wagging tails. She then indulged in her third cup of coffee and began to fume. The call had hurt her deeply. She felt that the group had done nothing more than support each other's talents in a very fair manner. This, apparently, was not how Eleanor saw it. As Rosalie was the only one to be contacted, it was up to her to present Eleanor's dissatisfaction and resignation to the group later that morning.

It was 11:00 a.m. when Rosalie mentioned her earlier

morning conversation—Eleanor's defection from and desertion of the Seven. The group's emotions were far more agitated than I could ever have imagined. I should have reminded myself that artists are a sensitive bunch and take every thought, emotion, and act to heart.

Lulu said, "I have tried to be supportive, even though I occasionally found her brush strokes weak."

Georgianna's response was, "You were a lot less critical of her painting than you were of mine!"

Angelique simply looked up to the ceiling of the building as if for divine guidance. Melissa continued to work on her happy merry-go-round scene. Rosalie was profoundly hurt, as she believed that she had been supportive and encouraging to Eleanor about her painting. She had shared her gallery contacts, as had the others. There seemed to be an unspoken code among these artists: if one seemed overly vulnerable or sensitive at a session, the critiques of that member's work would be few and between. Occasionally they would pull a "Sabine" and find the beautiful and unique in the mediocre.

Robin raised his eyebrows during these musings. He was tired of talk and dying to hit the canvas. So, typically of his Charles Dana Gibson style, he said, "Citizens, this is our call to arms."

Lulu moaned, "Oh, God, what now? Don't tell me there is going to be any violence. I am only armed with one sable brush."

Melissa, fast as a bolt of lightning, said, "I am going to replace the ponies on my carousel with war horses."

Angelique took down the Mona Lisa she had been working on, replaced it with a blank canvas, and began a sketch of St. George, sword in hand, slaying a dragon. She looked up at the skylight, noticed a little red insect prancing across it, and added it to her canvas.

Not to be outdone, Georgianna painted a wild boar into

the bucolic scene she was delineating. With palette knives and brushes in hand, and easels upright, the group of six continued to work with fresh spirits on their continuing quests for perfection.

My time is over here. I have observed a multitude of emotions, styles, and talents placed on canvases, many deserving better homes than a brick, former town garage on a brownfield. Although the circle is now smaller, it has gained strength in the shrinkage. My search shall continue as I observe from afar, hoping that I will find that human nature can change, and that history does not have to repeat itself.

JUDITH M. COOKE

Revival

Mama got saved again when the traveling preacher came to town. She gets saved every year under the big yellow tent set out at the fairgrounds. I've been saved four times myself. The tent revival is the best show that comes to Hawkins; it's even better than the carnival, and that has a Ferris wheel and a tent where you can see a two-headed piglet in a jar. Daddy doesn't mind us going to the tent revival as long as Mama doesn't give the preacher any money. Last year she gave him all our grocery money, and all we had to eat for the rest of the week was oatmeal and peanut butter sandwiches. This year he made her promise not to put anything in the collection place, and she did not put in a dime. She gave me the money, and I put it in. That way it's not a lie.

When we arrived at the revival, Mama sat down next to Mrs. Larson, who is her friend from church. They are both on the telephone prayer chain, which is how Mama keeps up with what's going on. Last week they were praying for Cindy Pearlson who wore a skirt that was too short for someone her age, and for Mr. Thomas who came home late and fell asleep drunk on his front lawn. Suzie Miller was sitting three rows behind us. She is in my Sunday School class, and she has a television in her bedroom. Mama wanted me to stay with her and Mrs. Larson, but I kept asking until she said fine, go sit with Suzie, just stop pestering me.

When the praise band started to play, we all stood up and sang *By the Blood of the Lamb; Savior, Redeemer, Friend;* and

Amazing Grace, How Sweet the Sound. Suzie's mom sang very loud, and she held her palms up like she was ready to catch the ceiling should the tent cave in. Three rows ahead, Mama was not singing the right words at all. She was interrupting the song, crying, "Praise you, Jesus! I just praise you, Jesus!" I was glad I was sitting with Suzie, who always sings the right words.

After the music, everyone sat down to hear what the preacher had to say. While he talked about sin and how he came to the Lord himself, Suzie and I tried to guess who would get saved that night. Mama and Mrs. Larson, definitely—they get saved every year. I said Mr. Fischer, because the prayer chain had noticed that he had been arguing with his wife. Suzie said Bobby Willis needed to get saved because he acted up in school so much no one could stand him except God. Suzie's mom said to pipe down and try to learn something from the sermon.

As the preacher talked, I liked to watch his teeth. They are all the exact same length and as white as an angel's robe. He dressed good, except his suit must have been too hot for him because his face was shiny with sweat, and he kept wiping his forehead with his handkerchief. At school, when the teacher talks, we have to be quiet, but in the tent when the preacher says the sermon, people yell things right out loud. "Amen!" "Praise you, Jesus!" "Lord, have mercy!" And he doesn't even seem to mind; he just talks louder. The louder he gets, the louder the people get, and Mama was the loudest one of all. "Thank you, Jesus! Thank you, Jesus!" she kept yelling over and over.

Then, we got to the best part. The preacher said that anyone who wanted to be right with God and needed saving should come forward. The praise band started playing again so the people could have some singing while they were finding salvation. Mrs. Larson was the first to make it to the altar, and Mama was close behind. Suzie's mom liked the singing so much she started dancing in the aisle, her eyes shut and her arms jiggling and her breasts bobbing to the music. A woman who drove in from another town caught the Holy Spirit so hard she fell backwards. Mama told me later that she was "slain in the Spirit," which I hope never happens to me, because she looked demon possessed, rolling on the ground in her flowered dress and muttering strange words.

As the people down front gave their lives to Jesus, the preacher got more and more excited, dancing and jumping around the stage. Every time another person came forward, he would pray at the top of his lungs, thanking God for his mercy. When I act like that at home, I get a time out, but in church it's okay because it means you got Jesus.

The music finally ended, and the revival was over. The band began packing up their instruments, and the people were saying their goodbyes and God-bless-yous.

Mama looked around, remembering that she had brought me with her. As we walked to the car, Mama was still blowing her nose. Her makeup was all smudged from crying. Her hair was sticking out, and her clothes looked like she'd slept in them all night.

"Are you okay, Mama?" I asked.

"Oh, yes Honey. I'm just fine!" she answered. "It's just so good to be right with God."

MICHAEL J. GORDON

Wendy And The Wise Guys

"**W**e need to come up with a good practical joke to play on Wendy," Harry Abrams declared.

Arthur Diggs and Hovey Banks, the two men seated next to him, nodded in mock somber agreement. They were not referring to a woman, but rather to their friend Wendell McGrath, who hated it when his friends called him Wendy.

"Something we haven't pulled before," mused Diggs.

Banks added, "Something that'll hit him where it hurts—like his wallet."

"Right," Abrams said, "People are beginning to think he and his money are surgically attached."

Wendell McGrath zealously guarded a carefully nurtured reputation as a cheapskate, even though his friends knew him to be a frequent contributor to worthy causes, where he insisted his donations be identified as "Anonymous" in any public listing.

"Hmm," they pondered. You could almost smell wood burning, as they say there in the mountains.

The three were lingering at a table in Bella's after the weekly meeting of the Chester's Landing Rotary Club. For years, the eatery had hosted the organization's Tuesday lunchtime meeting due to its being the only place in town with an extra dining room the club could temporarily claim as its own. After discarding several ideas as beneath their lofty standards of practical joking, the plotters settled on one which seemed promising.

When $1,000 is donated to the Rotary International Foundation, either by an individual or by someone else in that person's name, he or she receives recognition as a Paul Harris Fellow. The honor, named for the organization's founder, is a big deal within Rotary, and the Chester's Landing club typically donated that amount to the Foundation every year to recognize one of its members who had performed exemplary volunteer service.

The club traditionally awarded the medal and certificate that come with the honor at a special meeting in the middle of March. As the only scheduled public excitement between the end of skiing and the opening of fishing season, the event in the small upper New York State town usually drew a decent crowd. To build suspense, the name of each new recipient was kept secret until the presentation itself.

Of course, the selection committee knew the identity of the honoree, and since the current year's committee was comprised of the three men at the table, they all knew that this year it was to be Wendell McGrath.

When the president of the club announced his name at the awards ceremony—with the Rotary District Governor there to make the presentation—Wendell himself was completely taken aback. His face flush with surprise, he proudly accepted the honor to enthusiastic applause from the members and guests.

Now the plan devised by the three jokesters was set in motion. After letting Wendell enjoy his newfound status for a week, they went to the club treasurer, Jim Marini, the more-or-less permanent holder of the position as a result of his being the only Certified Public Accountant in Chester's Landing. They let him in on their scheme, and he eagerly agreed to go along with it.

"Attorney Diggs' office," a female voice cooed.
"Let me speak to Mr. Diggs."
"May I tell him who's calling?"
"Wendell McGrath."
Diggs answered. "Hi, Wendy (Diggs couldn't resist using that name). What can I do for you?"

"Artie, you got a Paul Harris Fellowship from the club last year. Did you get a bill for it afterward?"

"Sure, everyone does. Why?"

"Why? Because I got a bill for the one they gave me last week!" Diggs could visualize McGrath's face turning redder with every sentence. "How can they give you an award and then expect you to pay for it?"

"For God's sake, it's a charity, Wendy, and a darn good one. You do know that a hundred percent of Foundation funds goes for eleemosynary purposes, don't you?"

"Nuts to the Foundation, Artie, and nuts to you! And don't use those long lawyer words with me, either! Eleemosynary, my foot!" And he hung up on the smiling Arthur Diggs.

Next on Wendell's irate phone call list were Harry Abrams and Hovey Banks. Both gave him the same rehearsed answer. "Oh, yeah, I was billed when I got one, and paid gladly," each one attested. Hovey added that Wendell could pay in installments if he needed to, guessing (accurately) that among them all, Wendell had the least need to pay for anything in installments. McGrath hung up on each without saying good-bye.

The phone in Jim Marini's office rang bright and early the next morning. His secretary wouldn't be in for another fifteen minutes, so he answered it himself.

"Jim? Wendell. What's this bill I got from the club?"

"What bill?"

"From the Rotary Club! You sent it. You're the treasurer, for crying out loud!"

"How much was it for?" Jim played dumb to stretch out Wendell's agony.

"A thousand dollars!"

"Oh. That's for your Paul Harris Fellowship."

"I know that! It says so on the bill. But the club pays for the Paul Harris Fellowships it awards to members!" He paused slightly. "Doesn't it?"

"Only at first, so it can get the certificate and medal before the event. Didn't anyone tell you? The recipients then reimburse the club. They always have."

Wendell was getting agitated. "I'm not paying! I'll give the thing back first!"

"Can't do that, Wendell," Jim said. "The paperwork's been sent in. They'll kick you out of Rotary."

The phone went dead in the treasurer's hand.

Wendell worked his way up through the rest of the club officers, all of whom had by then been apprised of the situation. Each gave the same response: recipients always pay.

McGrath finally called the Rotary District Governor, to whom he delivered a long, agitated, stream-of-consciousness complaint about the two-faced, perfidious treachery of his club in not telling him ahead of time that he would have to pay.

"What are you talking about?" asked the surprised governor. "Your club never collects from its honorees."

Thus did Wendell learn of his friends' artful dodge. He confronted them at the next meeting.

"If you didn't nurture your image as a cheapskate so much," they replied, "you wouldn't be such a tempting target, Wendy."

"Don't call me Wendy!"

Things calmed down between Wendell and his friends afterward, but that didn't stop him from occasionally bellyaching about the affair. These complaints naturally prompted the three wise guys to idly dream of other scenarios. It had been over a year since the Paul Harris Fellowship episode, and thus high time to pull something else.

Inspired by an impending Space Shuttle launch, Artie Diggs had an idea.

They rented a helium tank, and purchased five hundred basketball-sized balloons, all yellow. Gathering to fill them inside Hovey Banks' small barn, they hung a paper tag from the knot as they tied off each one. It was slow going, and they needed the entire evening to get their plot off the ground. Their wives had been told not to wait supper, that they were ordering pizza from Bella's, and might not be home until late. It took them hours, but by 1:00 a.m. all the balloons had been filled with helium and tagged.

Then the barn doors were opened, and five hundred yellow balloons bobbed and floated high into the clear night sky above Chester's Landing.

Of course, what goes up must come down. Some fell to earth nearby, but prevailing winds took many across the Hudson River into Connecticut, Massachusetts, and the rest of New England. Several made it to Atlantic Canada, and one even rode the jet stream all the way to Iceland.

People who picked up the bright yellow, rubber remains from the ground found a small paper tag attached to each one. On the tag was an official-looking notice, which read:

ATTENTION

This balloon is part of a United States National Aeronautics and Space Administration (NASA) study to correlate actual wind patterns with computer projections. This is being done in preparation for launch of a new model Space Shuttle.

Should you find this tag, please call the following number anytime, 24 hours a day, and report the location at which it was found. If it is a toll call from your location, you may call collect.

The number listed was for Wendell McGrath's cell phone.

KENT JARRELL

A Path Not Taken

A MEMOIR

It was a London evening in the 1970s when I was shown in a flash what my life might have been, and what it was not going to be.

College friends from the University of Manchester and I spent as many weekends as possible in London, sharing a small, cheap apartment. We were escaping the boredom of the provincial and urban blighted Manchester for the excitement of the "Swinging City," which lingered on from the 1960s. Every evening we started out in pubs, where I learned to drink whiskey neat, and to hope for something better than greasy fish and chips wrapped in newspaper.

One Friday night, we elbowed up to the bar and started conversations with a group of young men dressed in formal wear, and fashionable Sloane Ranger women with their Hermes and Liberty silk head scarves worn just below their mouths.

By the end of a round of drinks, we found ourselves invited to a party at a nearby flat. A buffet awaited the glamorous and glossy before they headed out to a performance of the London Symphony Orchestra. We, the students dressed in turtleneck sweaters and pea coats, barely made the grade for admission to the pre-party but eagerly eyed the feast in the drawing room.

Emboldened by my standing as an expatriate in England, and by the drinks, I introduced myself to a more than attractive girl who was about my age. She asked, in what can only be described as upper class posh, "What doooo you doooo?"

She seemed interested in hearing my status as graduate

student abroad, working as an announcer on BBC radio, and, as I boasted, "weekending in London."

She chortled when I told her that part of my BBC duties included hosting "The Bangladeshi Hour." Every two weeks dozens of people from Manchester's Bangladeshi community would crowd into a cramped BBC studio to surround me in front of a single microphone. Some nights it would be political news and discussion. One night it was a live performance by a famous woman soloist I had never heard of from Dacca.

The singer immediately launched into 55 minutes of nonstop, high-pitched warbling that drove the standing room audience into ecstasy, and me into a throbbing headache. I was watching the clock closely as we approached the end time for the broadcast. There was no stopping the diva. I had to grab the microphone and quickly sign off, "Kent Jarrell for the BBC's Bangladeshi Hour," just as all three clock hands swept to the top of the hour. She sang on for another half hour. I was the only one who knew her harmonics were no longer being sent around the world on the BBC's bandwidth.

I kept my new party friend humorously engaged as I moved on to a tale about my hosting duties on the "At the Manchester Zoo" broadcast. I was in a cage with a tiger cub and the handler. Rolling tape, I narrated the story on my prized Uher tape recorder, a professional model purchased at a discount by a friend at the PX in Saigon. Everything was going well with the frisky young animal, named Obo, while the handler animatedly described the cat's background and feeding habits. Suddenly, the handler's voice dropped a couple of octaves and he said coolly, "That's enough. Drop your hands. Look away from Obo. Back away. Slowly. Get behind me."

He pointed to the tiger's paws. Claws, small, but very sharp, had popped out. I did as ordered and also closed my eyes. I figured if I couldn't see Obo, Obo couldn't see me. The handler calmed Obo down and shoved me, unharmed, out of the cage.

When the piece played on BBC radio, the absolute fear in my

voice was clear and palpable to those listening.

Overhearing my self-centered stories at the party was an older man who described himself as the London bureau chief for Reuters News Service. He asked how I had ended up working, on air, for the BBC? I told him of my apprentice work in the states as a reporter and of my plans to attend a graduate journalism program at Northwestern University. To my surprise, he said that we must get together. He wanted to talk to me about coming on at Reuters to get firsthand international experience, instead of wasting time with more class work.

The girl was at my side, listening, and moving, I thought, ever closer. I was feeling quite urbane. I turned to her, offered my arm, and said, "Why don't we step into the next room where we can have another glass of wine?"

She smiled. We turned together. I nodded sagely at the man from Reuters and strode to a line of wine bottles sitting on a finely textured white tablecloth on a table sitting on a white rug.

"Red?" I asked.

"Bordeaux, please," she said.

In a gesture of self-assuredness, I picked up a corkscrew and twisted it into the bottle. Instantly, the bottom of the bottle blew out, spewing blood red wine over the tablecloth, onto the rug, and across the front of her dress. She looked like she had been shot. Startled and wide eyed, she stepped back.

Suddenly we were not alone in the room. Her friends raced over and, armed with cloth napkins, began to daub at her dress as they ushered her away from me. A man, who I quickly figured out was the owner of the flat, demanded, "Who are you?"

Apparently, my answer was not satisfactory. I found myself escorted towards the front door. Over my shoulder, I waved to the man from Reuters and said, "I can call you Monday."

There had been a turn of fortune. As I was given the bum's rush out, I heard his reply, "Not so sure. Not really any availabilities at Reuters for you. Good night and good luck."

There I was, on a damp, dark London street, alone. My

friends back inside wisely decided that there was no value in rushing to my defense.

It all had seemed so close. The girl, the job, and an entree to the superiority of the British upper class. Right in my hands.

I shook my head. I still had a few pounds in my pocket so I walked back to the pub for a brooding pint of bitter. The evening had presented a shining path not taken, but the choice had not been mine.

JAMES E. McKIE, JR.

Incident on the Elwha

A MEMOIR

We were driving east on US 101 headed for Port Angeles, Washington when we saw the first one. On the side of the road, a small white sign was doing its job—it caught our attention. On its white surface were the words, EVER DONE THE ELWHA? As we came out of the next curve, there was another sign, NO? WHY NOT? Around the next bend was ELWHA RIVER RAFTING—2 MILES. Our ten-year-old son, Darrin, began reading each sign's words out loud. Soon it became a game—who could read the next one first? By the time we reached the sign, ELWHA RIVER RAFTING—NEXT LEFT, my wife and I had decided two things: our son's distance vision was much better than ours, and we wanted to stop and ask about rafting the Elwha. So, at the large black arrow, I took a left.

Barbara, my wife of nineteen years, Darrin, and I entered a large rustic building where we were greeted by a man in his twenties.

"Hi folks, are you here for the eleven o'clock trip?"

I explained that the three of us were there to get information, had no rafting experience, and hadn't yet decided if we wanted to go rafting. After a few questions about our vacation and interests, he suggested a private tour—a half-day raft trip with an expert guide. The trip would just be our guide and us, and the cost covered all gear and snacks. There was one available that day, at one o'clock, with one of their guides, Lindsey. Barb asked about the trip's cost. It was twenty dollars per adult and ten dollars for children ten and under.

Hearing that, Darrin sang out, "Daddy, pleeeese let's take the trip!"

I smiled at the young man and handed him my credit card.

"Be here thirty minutes before departure to get ye suited up," were his parting words.

The summer day was near perfect, eighty degrees and low humidity. We had an early lunch of sandwiches from our ice chest at a picnic table next to the beautiful Elwha River. Our map showed that the river arose in the snow-covered mountains of Olympic National Park and, for forty-five miles, wound north through rugged canyons, finally entering the Strait of Juan de Fuca. A brochure said it was a river that had very cold water all year, because almost all of it came from melting glacial ice and snow. All three of us were so excited to go that we showed up at the check-in area fifty minutes early.

We were measured and given our gear: red rain jacket and pants, black rubber boots, yellow life vest, and red hardhat. I signed a waiver saying the raft company wasn't responsible for any injury or death on the trip. We were then directed to a van where our guide was waiting.

"Hi, I'm Lindsey, your captain for today's run."

After introductions and small talk, Lindsey announced that she was driving us to the put-in place, where our raft, on the van's roof, would be launched. Once on the river, she'd give us safety and paddling instructions.

The Elwha River at the put-in place was wide and its water flowed gently. As we exited the van, Lindsey looked at me and said, "Jim, help me get this raft down and haul it to the floating dock."

After donning our life vests, Lindsey told us where to sit in the red rubber raft. Our designated positions were: Barb at the right side, Jim at the left side, and Darrin at the bow. Lindsey handed Barb and me each a paddle and placed her paddle at the stern.

Next came the safety instructions, "Keep life vests on at all times when in the raft," "Smoking is not permitted in the raft," and "No standing in the raft during the trip."

Lindsey then climbed into the stern, untied the raft and pushed us out on the river. Now, the paddle instructions:

With an authoritative tone, Lindsey proclaimed, "Paddling is not optional on this tour. In order to navigate this river's rapids, I'll need your help. If I say, 'more Jim' that means increase your strokes-a-minute, Jim, and if I say, 'more Barb', well, you get the picture."

We meekly nodded, and began practicing, Lindsey steering the raft left and right from the stern, and Jim and Barb taking orders at the sides.

After about ten minutes practicing, Lindsey said, "You passed the test, now let's go have fun."

We paddled off downriver. Everything was going very smoothly as we navigated small patches of white water. Little by little, the banks of the river closed in and the river picked up speed. Before long, the river's narrowing accelerated and we began to hear a faint rumbling noise ahead.

I asked Lindsey if that was thunder, to which she replied, "No, that's the Boulder Garden rapids, a fun part of this trip today."

I thought, *Boulder Garden? —That doesn't sound like fun.* Ahead, a sharp bend in the river prevented us seeing what we were hearing and the noise from around the bend was getting very loud.

As we came through the turn, the Elwha became a roaring explosion of sound that made it difficult to hear. Worse yet, the sight of the Boulder Garden was absolutely frightening. Four-foot, white water waves were smashing between huge boulders, and we were quickly losing control of the raft. Lindsey was screaming orders while Barb and I were doing our best to hear her, when suddenly the raft went sideways. Luckily, Darrin had left the bow and was now, between Barb and me, holding onto the back of our life vests.

What happened next was a nightmare. The raft hit a six-foot tall boulder, slid halfway up its nearly vertical side, wrapping its red rubber self around it. The raft became motionless because the weight of all the water it had taken on was effectively super-gluing it to the columnar boulder. We were hung up and going nowhere. While none of us were thrown out into the rapids, we were in trouble—we three adults were up to our knees in frigid water that was almost up to Darrin's waist. We adults had our backs against the boulder and managed to squirm to a standing position, balancing with both feet on the edge of the raft that was out of the water. I pulled Darrin up, placing his feet by mine. All four of us now had our feet mostly out of the water, minimizing the chances of hypothermia.

In stark contrast to the calm and stoic way we three were dealing with our situation, Lindsey screamed at Barbara and me, blaming us for what had happened. I finally told her, "SHUT UP, and start thinking about what to do next."

Her reply was, "Hey Jim, I'm in charge. Cut me some slack, this is my first summer as a rafting guide, but I'll think of something."

That's when we learned that Lindsey wasn't the experienced guide we'd been told would captain our raft.

I soon learned that thinking rationally was not Lindsey's forte. Her first, and only, order was, "Jim climb to the top of our boulder and then jump to the next boulder, and so on, until you reach the shore and run for help."

I tried explaining to her that there was no way that I could do that, because the boulder was covered entirely with slimy green algae. If, by some miracle, I reached its top, I would then have to execute a standing jump of some eight feet, landing on the top of the adjacent boulder that was also covered with the same algae. I also pointed out that, between these two green monoliths, there was a roaring hole to eternity, waiting to catch me should I slip and drop between them. Simply put, it was suicide. The bottom line—neither Barb nor I could convince

Lindsey that her plan wasn't feasible. I finally gave up and said, "Lindsey, if you think it makes sense, then you do it!"

Barb turned to me at that point and said, "Good for you, Jim."

Minutes later, Darrin's great eyesight saved the day when he spotted a fisherman upriver about a hundred-fifty yards away. We all started waving our arms at him and finally got his attention. We knew he saw us, because he waved back and returned to fishing. Exasperated, we frantically waved and waved. Thankfully, when we got his attention again, he finally got the message. He ran off, climbed a steep switchback trail to the canyon's top, and disappeared from sight.

For what seemed like hours, we waited for something to happen. And, finally, something did. We heard it before we saw it—the rhythmic rumble of a helicopter's big, horizontal blade. It grew louder and suddenly the chopper came into view. More importantly, it was headed our way. As it got closer, we could clearly see it was carrying beneath it what looked like a large cage. A cage for us? we thought. Our hopes were dashed when it flew right over us and never returned. Lindsey was sobbing and saying, "No one's coming to rescue us, we're all doomed."

After another hour or so, we were startled by a voice coming from high above. Had we died and God was calling us? Well, sort of, it was a godsend to be sure, we heard a stocky man in a uniform who stood at the canyon rim about fifty feet above the river and some two hundred feet from us. He spoke through a yellow bullhorn, and, despite the roar of the rapids, his high-pitched voice could be clearly heard, "Man in the raft, raise one arm for yes, two for no. Do you understand what I said?"

I raised one arm.

"Is anyone badly injured?"

I raised both arms.

"Great, now listen closely. We will get you all out of that raft, one person at a time. A rope line will be shot your way. Man in the raft, you are to grab the rope as it moves past the raft. Do not, I repeat, do not try to grab it unless it's within easy reach. Understand?"

One of my arms went up. The next sound we heard was a loud boom as the rope was shot from what sounded like a cannon. The rope line missed the raft by some twenty feet and was pulled back up. A second shot got it a lot closer, but still not easily reachable. The third shot was right on target, but I underestimated the rope's speed and missed grabbing it. On the fourth attempt, I caught it and heard, "Man in the raft, wrap the rope four times around your waist and then grip the rope tightly with both hands. When you're set, give us a yes and we'll tighten the rope from our end."

After wrapping the heavy rope around my middle, I shot one arm up and the rope became taut.

"Man in the raft, prepare to receive our Easter basket. Mother of the boy, when the basket arrives, bring it into the raft and place your son in it, then lock him in with the harness belt. Understood?"

Barb raised one arm. The basket soon appeared, hanging beneath the rope via a wheeled pulley device to which was attached a second rope line.

"Mom, wouldn't it be cool if the basket had had a big chocolate bunny in it for us?"

Barb couldn't help replying, "It sure would be, my funny, brave boy."

As instructed, she grabbed the basket, placed it next to Darrin, and helped him into it. After he was seated, cross-legged, she placed the harness around his shoulders and waist and locked it in place. Barb then said, "Darrin, don't be afraid, before long, you'll be safely up there, wrapped in a warm blanket." She kissed him, raised her arm, and the basket was pulled up and away from the raft. Hanging beneath the main rope, the basket was slowly pulled back up by the rescue team manning the second rope line. We couldn't be prouder of the brave little boy who took that ride up to the rim, without a whimper or a tear.

"Mother of the boy, get ready for your ride in the basket," came the command from above. "After you're locked in and ready to be pulled up, give us a one-arm salute." Barb did as instructed and was soon on her way back up to join Darrin. As Barb-in-the-basket began to rise, she looked down at me, blew me a kiss, and said, "See you in a few minutes, Sweetie."

Now, as the basket was slowly being returned, Lindsey loudly proclaimed, "I'm a woman, and I'm the next one to get saved."

I was about to say, "Have a nice ride, captain," but bit my tongue instead. And, as the bitch-in-the-basket was rising to the rim, I suddenly thought, so, how am I going to get rescued? Soon, my question was answered—a young guy, wearing a black hardhat, black wet suit, and black flippers, who looked a bit like a seal, was approaching from upstream. He was riding the rapids on a surfing board. He arrived at the raft and released me from my rope cummerbund, wrapping it around his waist.

After watching the basket procedure three times, I was a pro, soon being safely returned to Barb and Darrin. Actually, arriving at the rim provided an unexpected surprise—so many rescue vehicles from Elwha Town, Port Angeles, and the National Park Service. After cleaning us up a bit and exams by a doctor, we were deemed to have survived the scary adventure and were told that we would probably live to ripe old ages, filled with lots more "adventures." We thanked the bullhorn-wielding chief and his crew for rescuing us.

Someone drove us back to Elwha River Rafting where we got a full refund and three, free Elwha River tee shirts. I don't recall anyone asking us questions about our ordeal. We were so thankful to be alive, that we forgot to register a complaint about Lindsey, who was nowhere to be found. I'd like to believe that an investigation took place after we left and that the rafting company and Lindsey were held responsible.

A good amount of time passed before we tried a white water trip again. Seven years later, in 1991, we finally returned to river running when the three of us braved all the Colorado River's monster rapids on a trip through the Grand Canyon. It was an awesome, two-week adventure during which, incidentally, we didn't have to paddle once.

Oh, about that helicopter, we later found out that its pilot was not looking for us. The pilot was assigned to remove feral goats, not rescue river rafters in peril!

RAE STUDHOLME

Ferry's Funeral Home

My mother does dead people's hair. It's a job she's inordinately fond of. Her voice swells with pride when she speaks of it. "Not just anybody can get into it these days," she gloats. "The funeral parlors, they're sewed up tight. They've even got waiting lists. People are dying for this job!" she says without irony. "It took me years to get into Ferry's and now that I'm pals with all the guys there, the embalmers, I'll never leave. They've promised me a good deal on my funeral. They'll just have to wheel me out of there."

She sips her highball, removes her shoes, and lights a Newport cigarette.

My mother keeps her supplies in the trunk of her car, a 1965 sky-blue, push-button-gearshift Rambler. The trunk is packed with curling irons, bobby pins, cans of Aqua Net hairspray, combs floating in formaldehyde. When she opens the door, the car emits the faint aroma of menthol and embalming fluid. The scents are quickly masked by her Estee Lauder Youth Dew perfume.

"It's all I use on them," she says. "None of this blow dryer stuff. After all, they're dead and I only have to style the front and sides. Comb all their hair to the front. Unless, of course, they wear an upsweep. Then all bets are off. Wigs are the easiest. Just fix them up and slip them on. I go by the pictures the family shows me. That's the way they like it, and that's the way I do it."

My mother wears a uniform to work. A white dress. White shoes. All that's missing is the starched white nurse's cap. She's even got a blue cape. She wears this erstwhile nurse's uniform unselfconsciously. "I'm a professional, and I have to dress like one," she says as she walks to the Rambler in a haze of perfume.

My mother invites me to accompany her to the morgue. She wants to fix me up with one of the young morticians. He's still only an apprentice, but my mother sees him as a great catch.

"He'll always have a good paying job," she tells me. "And at least one nice black suit." I wait in the car.

My mother has living customers, too. She calls them her "seniors." I call them her blue-haired set.

"My seniors like their permanent waves. Every three months they need one. Wash and sets once a week. Some of them still ask for finger waves. It's the blue rinses I hate. That dye stays on my hands for days. I've tried using surgical gloves. Don't understand how doctors can use them. Can't feel a thing with those on. I try to talk my ladies into going blonde. Like me."

Our house holds the smell of hairspray, dye and permanent wave solution like a cherished memory of the holy trinity. It's better than the formaldehyde, I suppose.

But my mother disagrees. It's the funeral home clients she adores. She is particularly boastful when she gets a special request. This usually happens when one of her blue-haired ladies dies.

"Hazel even left it in her will that I was the only one who could fix her hair in the casket. That Hazel was a fussy one. And pushy to boot. She always gets her way. Even when she's dead."

My mother does dead people's hair, but she never talks about death. For her it's, all about the hair and looking good at the end.

In the end, she wants to be cremated. No one could ever do her hair to suit her.

PAULA SPURLIN PAIGE

Gluten and Other Abominations

A long black hair from the mane of the baroque soprano snaked across the kitchen sink, which I'd just cleaned. I hate these damn musicians! Especially the lutenist, who goes into rages if anyone leaves the lid off his precious little metal box of Lapsang Souchong. He also persists in leaving the toilet seat up, which I find offensive to women, and he's a food snob. Pesto should have pine nuts in it, he said, after I'd made it without, because the damn things are so expensive. Not always, I'd said. The old recipes don't have pine nuts. His eyebrows zipped up his high forehead, as if I didn't know my business as a caterer.

And then, the food restrictions of this snotty little group! The soprano can't eat raw onions; the actress is a strict vegan, who thinks that drinking milk is as bad as eating meat (because you're raping the cow!); another won't eat gluten and wants everything bland and well-cooked; someone else likes everything raw, so that it's almost impossible to make one meal that everyone can sit down and eat civilly together.

After one particularly disastrous dinner, during which the soprano claimed to have ingested a piece of raw onion in her potato salad—although I had made hers specifically for her—I slapped the crème brûlée (no eggs, no dairy, disgusting!) on the table so loudly they all looked at me. Then I took refuge in the library with a glass of red wine. The owner of the place, which was a sort of art center, found me taking big swigs and deep breaths when he came through after dinner.

"Sorry," Alex said, as he sat down beside me. "I know, they

can be a big pain in the butt, can't they?"

"Yeah." I was surprised that he could see right through me.

"Spoiled trust fund kids, most of them," he said, smiling. He was an attractive man in his sixties, bald, with warm blue eyes.

"Really?"

"Wait a minute." He went to the kitchen, came back with a glass of wine for himself and closed the door. "Well, not Megan. The actress. She's just crazy. Not sure why she's here. But most people in early music have money."

"They do? Why is that?"

"I guess because they wouldn't go into it otherwise. There's not much demand for their services. Not many baroque concerts."

I sipped my wine and looked at him. "Oh."

He frowned at me. "You look tired, Annie. How's business?"

I shrugged. "Not great. Hasn't been much of a year. A few weddings, mostly gays."

He smiled. "They're the only ones who want to get married now, huh?"

"I guess."

"How's Eric?"

"He's doing all right." The thought of my husband made me tear up for a moment. To distract myself, I said: "And what is it with this gluten thing? People have been eating wheat for thousands of years. All of a sudden, every other person thinks they can't eat it."

We both started to giggle.

"You can't let them upset you," Alex said, looking at me calmly. He rummaged in his pocket and handed me an actual handkerchief. "I know, it's harder for you, because you have to deal with their nutty food phobias, but believe me, they get to me, too. We both have to put up with a lot of shit, because we need money. Sure, I'd rather be up here by myself, but I have to rent this place out to musical groups and such a few weeks a summer or I couldn't pay the taxes."

"Oh," I said. "Sorry."

"Don't be. Week after next I've got a yoga workshop. You interested in catering that?"

I tried not to sigh. "Sure. If they're not all vegans."

Alex smiled. "Relax. You need to get out more, Annie. All work and no play makes Annie a dull girl."

"How am I supposed to get out? I'm always working."

"Right now we could go to Brio's, have a drink. Leave your car off at home on the way, tell Eric, then I'll drop you off on the way back."

"Well…"

"Come on." He pulled me up.

"I haven't put the dishes in the dishwasher."

"I'll do it in the morning."

We walked out around the trust fund babies, who seemed to be discussing some thorny musical subject. The actress was studying her green fingernails. They all looked up at the two of us together in surprise, probably because they thought of me as the help.

The road to Phoenicia wound slowly down the mountain. Alex took it pretty fast, so I tried to keep up with him. I'm from New York, like a lot of people up here, and I didn't even drive until we moved up here fulltime ten years ago, when our son was twelve. I remembered what a funk Tim was in, screaming that we were ruining his life by taking him away from his friends in the city and plunging him into this wilderness. I was scared, too, scared of the isolation, of bears, of having to learn to drive at thirty-nine before I could even look for a job. I got used to it, but I still find nature pretty wild and scary, particularly at night. The headlights catch glistening little eyes staring out at you. Deer nestle in the underbrush, and may decide to bolt out in front of you at anytime. I'd hit a doe once, going home at night, and had almost lost control of the car. This time, the wild critters all stayed put, and I sighed in relief when we got to our rambling old house by the road in Chichester. It was a vacation cottage that we'd built on to and had winterized.

I walked through the kitchen, where the table and nearly every available surface was covered with cookbooks, novels and mail—the last because I'm on the list of every leftwing cause in the country.

In our room Eric was sitting up in bed, bare-chested in the heat, watching a video. His cane, an elaborately-carved reproduction of an old Catskills walking stick, stood by the bed.

"Hi, honey," he said, smiling and patting the bed beside him. "You're early."

I sat down on the edge of the bed. "I'm not through yet. Alex wants to talk to me about a wedding. We're going to Phoenicia." I couldn't manage to tell him that I just had to get out.

He made his funny face, in which he purses his lips and scowls. "I'm sorry you have to work so hard."

I leaned over and kissed him and ruffled his grayish-blond hair. He looked completely normal, as though he were waiting for me in bed the way he always has, when I have to work late.

"I'm free all day tomorrow," I said.

"Good." He switched the VCR back on, which I took as a cue to leave.

Alex and I drove on to Phoenicia. It was Saturday night, so Main Street was jumping. We parked over by Mama's Boy, then walked to Brio's. The outside tables were all taken, and, as we worked our way in, we saw that the inside ones were, too.

"Damn," Alex said. A waitress motioned in the direction of the bar. "That's going to be even louder. Do you mind?"

"No," I said, although I did, thinking I'd like to keep what's left of my hearing.

We wove our way into the bar and sat down at a table in a corner a few feet away from the counter. The noise was deafening. I caught a glimpse of myself in the mirror over the bar, saw that my shoulder-length brown hair had gone noodle-limp in the humidity and that I looked grim with no makeup. I tried smiling, and the effect was better. A woman at the bar with pulled-back blond hair smiled back, apparently thinking that I'd been smiling at her.

I ordered a Marguerita. Then I noticed that the bar was packed with women. "What is this, Ladies Night Out?"

Alex began to chuckle. "You really don't get out much, do you?"

"I told you. I haven't been out in a year."

"Saturday night is lesbian night in Phoenicia."

"Of course." I began to laugh.

The Margueritas arrived, and we tried to have a conversation over the din.

"Is Eric able to work at all?"

"Well, he's started to make furniture. Turns out he's always wanted to be a cabinetmaker, and he's good at it. He's sold a couple of pieces."

"But he's not... he's sold the antique business?"

"It's on the market. Too much lifting. And standing. He can't do that anymore."

"That's tough. But he still lectures?"

"If he doesn't have to travel too far."

He looked at me steadily for a few seconds. Perhaps he was feeling sorry for me because I was now the chief breadwinner, and a glorified cook at that, but it was more likely he was thinking of sex. People have been looking at me like that for the past year, ever since Eric had his stroke. At first, I never thought about it. I was just glad he was alive, happy to cuddle with him and no more. We've been married for over twenty years, with one son. Physically, Eric's all right down there, and the doctor cleared him for sex. But when we start, he stops when he gets really excited and then just concentrates on me. He's afraid, it's obvious. But we can't seem to talk about it. There must be something I can do to help him, but damned if I know what it is.

The joint was jumping. It wasn't just the ladies at the bar. Kids shrieking in the dining room. Waitresses passing with loaded trays, flirting with the bartender. Somewhere under it all there was music, but it was impossible to tell what. We started to talk about Alex's career—he's a violist—but I could hardly hear him. Something about the difficulties for musicians in the Catskills, Woodstock impossible, opportunities at Glimmerglass drying up for some reason. Finally, we gave up and nursed our drinks. Then he excused himself and headed for the men's room.

I sat and felt sorry for myself, glancing occasionally at the bar, at the laughing women, who were obviously having a good time. Serves you right, some impudent voice said in my head. Sex was one thing we'd never had to worry about—it just happened like clockwork. Sure, I'd lost some libido with menopause, but Eric sure hadn't. I remembered our trip to Rome several years before, after a bumper year of antique sales. We'd had an argument by the Tiber because, he said, I was such a damn tourist—all I wanted to do was go out and see old stones when we were in one of the most romantic places in the world. His idea of a vacation was to spend the morning in bed making love, not trudging through the Forum in the hot Roman sun. We'd sat there so long that a scam artist had walked by a couple of times, asking for money to fill his gas tank so he could get back to Paris. We'd ended up laughing and going back to the hotel to bed.

I studied the women at the bar, wondering idly if life was any easier with a woman. Lots of short hair, of course, but not on all of them. Like the woman who'd smiled at me. She had strawberry-blond hair, probably her own color, tied up in a ponytail. She was drinking her beer, deep in conversation with the woman next to her. But then she looked over at me, smiling when she saw I was looking at her. The next thing I knew she'd hopped off the barstool and was on her way over to my table.

"Hi," she said, standing there in white shorts and a blue tank top that clung to her very shapely breasts. Youngish, late thirties, maybe forty. She looked me over and said:

"Why don't you ditch the old guy and come with us?"

I couldn't help laughing. "He's not old. But if he's old, then so am I." This wasn't really true, because Alex was probably at least ten years older than me.

She shook her head, and her ponytail switched around. "You're not old. You have beautiful eyes."

"Listen, I'm not…"

"Gay? You can say it." After a moment: "You know, most women are bi."

"Not me." I smiled. "I'm very happy with my husband."

"Oh. You mean… him?" She nodded toward the bathrooms in the back. "Sorry for what I said."

"No, he's a client."

"You know, you look familiar. What do you do?"

"Catering," I said, wondering why I was continuing the conversation, but it was sort of fun.

She grinned. "That's it. Didn't you cater Sally Herman's wedding?"

I nodded.

"I'm Carrie," she said, stretching out her hand to take mine.

"Annie."

I tried to avoid her gaze by looking around for Alex, who could come back at any time. But I ended up noticing her white throat, and the curve of her breasts that were just above my eye level, since I was sitting down. So, I looked up and met her eyes. It was nice to have someone looking at me so attentively, even if it was a woman. What would it be like…? I felt like I was blushing, that a wave of heat was forking through me.

Fortunately, Alex came back just then, and Carrie went back to the bar, tossing me a smile over her shoulder.

He gave me a tongue-in-cheek grin as he sat down. "Sorry. Did I interrupt something?"

"Probably a good thing you did. It's the first time a woman has ever come on to me."

"I'm surprised. You're an attractive woman, and there are a lot of lezzies up here."

We tried to continue our conversation, but the noise was getting louder, so we left. Carrie waved a nonchalant goodbye.

In the car I started to laugh, peels of laughter that sailed out through the open windows and made the people walking on the sidewalk on this festive Saturday night turn around and look at us as we drove past.

"Well, guess I was right to take you out," Alex said. "You're forgotten all about the trust fund kids, haven't you?"

"Yes, I guess so." I managed to stop laughing, but I was still smiling.

We started back up the mountain, through the summer night. I noticed sounds I hadn't heard coming down here, like the wonderful August drone of the cicadas. A breeze had sprung up, ruffling the leaves of the big old-growth trees on both sides of the road. Somehow, I'd shed the stress and fatigue that usually weighed me down by the weekend. I didn't feel like an old lady anymore. Actually, I was feeling horny. A plan was taking shape in my mind.

"So, you won't need me tomorrow?" I asked Alex as I got out.

"No, can't afford it. I'll make them pasta. Gluten-free, of course."

Our little house was dark, except for the light in the bedroom at the back of the house. I went into the hallway and rooted around in the bottom drawer of a bureau where I kept out of season clothes until I found my old Victoria's Secret nightgown. It was white, demure and made of cotton, unlike the sleazy stuff they stock now. I slipped out of my sundress and underwear and put it on.

There was no video noise from the bedroom. I was afraid Eric was asleep. But when I went to the door, there he was, still sitting up in bed, reading a copy of "Maine Antiques Digest." He grinned when he saw me.

"Hi. Haven't seen that one in a while."

I realized that I hadn't been very attentive about my bedtime appearance since his stroke—I'd taken to wearing ratty flannel pajamas, since it's usually cool at night up here, even in the summer. So maybe I wasn't helping the situation, either.

Eric looked happier than he had when I went out. I noticed that there was a copy of his monograph on the Hudson Valley painters on the bedside table, which I hadn't seen for a while.

"Tim called," he said.

"How is he?"

"Fine. He's spending the weekend with a girl named Susan in Point Reyes."

"Where's that?"

"North of San Francisco. Job's going well."

"He's all grown up. A job and a girl. What else is there?"

"And"—Eric waved a letter in the air—"they've asked me to talk on Cole at the Clark Museum in November."

"That's great. See, things are going to work out."

"How about a glass of wine?"

When I went out to get it, I put Ella Fitzgerald singing "Embraceable You" on the CD player, turned down low. He was smiling when I came back in, as though he could see through my subterfuge.

"None for you?"

"I just had a Marguerita at Brio's."

His smile disappeared. "Brio's? You went to talk business at Brio's? You can't hear yourself think there, much less talk."

"Alex thought I needed a drink. I was upset about his current bunch of Juilliard brats."

Eric's greenish eyes bored into me. "Should I be concerned about your friendship with him?"

"Of course not." I sat down on the bed, hoping this wasn't going to get us off course. "He has a girlfriend. And I have you. And I knew you wouldn't want to go to Brio's on a Saturday night."

"Fair enough." He reached over and pulled me to him. "Of course you need to have a life. I know this period has been tough for you, too. And you've been very patient with me."

We smiled at each other and kissed. He sighed and set down his wine glass. I laid my head on his chest while he stroked my hair. He smelled of Ivory soap, a barely perceptible scent that took me back to my childhood. I smelled like the coconut milk and the seaweed flakes I'd put in the damn crème brûlée, but he didn't seem to mind. Then the old chemistry took over, and we made love just as we used to before the stroke. Gently at first, and then passionately. The fear had gone.

And he didn't die.

Originally published in *Stirring: A Literary Magazine.* © 2016

JUDITH BANNON SNOW

How Not to Buy a Dog

A MEMOIR

In the early summer of 1976, we were looking for a large houseplant—a dracaena or maybe a philodendron. Some friends told us that a local pet store was selling large (five to six feet) healthy houseplants for less than twenty dollars. All five of us—me, the ex, and the kids—went to check out the plants. While there, John, Kathryn, and Aaron spotted a darling puppy in a small cage against the wall. They wanted to let the whimpering (begging, really) little puppy out of her cage. The little thing was a Siberian Husky, so cute that we all wanted to pet her, even though we had no intention of getting a dog.

In the center of the pet store, a round wooden enclosure surrounded with benches could seat about six to eight people. We entered through the gate and sat down. The clerk brought the puppy into the enclosure and shut the gate. She went wild with excitement, loving the freedom and the attention. She had one brown eye and one blue eye, perky ears, and a curly tail. After instantaneously bonding with the dog, the children couldn't stand the idea of putting her back in her small wire cage, and begged to keep her.

Houseplants were forgotten as we pulled out the credit card, bought the dog, the food, the water dish, a collar, and a leash. We decided to name her Sappho. She lived up to her name, being incredibly independent, wayward, and fearless.

What we didn't know at the time was that she was a 'puppy mill' dog. Growing up, my mother made sure we always had a dog, but we never purchased one—our dogs were either strays or 'used' dogs that others couldn't keep or didn't want. Given my limited dog history, I was unaware of the problems with overbreeding.

It turns out she was the best of dogs and the worst of dogs. I believe that to be true of Siberian Huskies, in general, and Sappho in particular.

They are so friendly, but look (and can be) scary. Sappho could take down a raccoon in a heartbeat. She also killed a neighbor's little kitten when the kids were taking her for a walk. Awful. Also, Siberians don't bark, they howl. But Sappho was a quick learner and we taught her to bark, which she would do on command.

A Siberian is a beautiful dog to behold—tail high and what looks like a smile on its face. They hate being penned or tied up, love to roam, and are hard to catch. Early on, Sappho discovered that we couldn't outrun her, and if she didn't wish to come when called, she didn't have to. This led to many unpleasant experiences, both when we caught her and when we didn't.

No one was home weekdays until the kids came back from school or daycare. Our house had a wooded area that included a large dog pen with an enclosed shelter. She would cry and howl all day when left in the pen. It was heartbreaking, and even worse when we tied her on a lead. So we often let her roam, either because we couldn't catch her in the morning or because she was despondent and depressed when she was tied or penned.

When she was still a puppy, the next-door neighbors accused Sappho of leading their aged Bassett Hound astray. Other neighbors, farther up the street, used to lure her into their kitchen (as I said, Siberians are very friendly) and tell my tearful kids they would never see her again. Another time, a man had found her several miles from home and threatened to keep her because we were irresponsible dog owners. She was much admired, and many people wanted to keep her. She was also very friendly with the dogcatcher and eagerly jumped into his truck, never learning her lesson. We got tickets, paid fines, and got her back.

One time, while glancing through our weekly town newspaper, I saw my name listed as having been arrested for letting my dog roam—definitely news to me. This section of the weekly newspaper was prone to hyperbole. Nothing ever came of it, and I never chose to follow up on my 'arrest.' Some time later, Sappho made the paper yet again. This time she was lingering by the bike racks at the middle school waiting for the kids to get out. For some reason, whenever she was photographed, she would yawn. The staff photographer took her picture and, on cue, she yawned. The caption in the paper was "Dog bored at school."

We estimated Sappho's birthday to be April 23, 1976 and celebrated it each year. During the first months, we took her to the Guilford Veterinary Clinic regularly. When she was eleven months old, our favorite vet told us that Sappho had juvenile cataracts. We cried. Our sweet little puppy couldn't see. It was the first manifestation of the puppy mill syndrome.

We took her to the dog ophthalmologist at Yale (who knew Yale had a dog ophthalmologist?) He confirmed the diagnosis. In 1977, vets couldn't or wouldn't perform cataract surgery on dogs—it was not presented as an option. The ophthalmologist said that she could see light and dark, but not much else. He told us that dogs don't depend much on vision—scent and hearing were much more important. Sappho did manage to have a mostly happy life, although she could never catch a tennis ball or a frisbee. Later in life, she did run into a car in the street in front of our house. She was not hurt, but the motorist was frantic.

Sappho loved the snow. At the first snowfall of the year, she would run through the drifts using her nose as a plow. After she tired, she would find a comfy snowdrift, curl up in a ball, and take a nap. She was very fluffy and never seemed to get cold.

The summer was another matter. One hazy, hot, and humid ninety-five degree day, we decided to give her an outdoor bath.

We washed her down with shampoo and rinsed her with the hose. Our formerly fluffy dog looked like a scrawny rat. We tried to dry her with towels, to no avail. She shivered for hours trying to get warm. It was her first, and last, bath.

When Sappho was ten or so, the cruciate ligaments in her hind legs failed. The vet said he could manufacture a brace by sewing her skin into a ridge. As it healed, it would create a scar that would stabilize her legs. She would have an overnight stay at the vet. Total cost of her surgery and hospital stay—only one hundred dollars. Wow. I asked him if he would be willing to see my children. He said no.

In 1987, when my husband at the time left the family, Sappho started coming into the house on her own. It could have been her advancing age, but I don't think so. From the time she was a puppy, when my now ex-husband was in the house, she would not willingly come in. We used to tempt, catch, and cajole her to come in for the night. The yelling, turmoil, and anger in our home terrified her. After the ex left, she became an integral part of our family. My two grown kids came home to live with my teenage youngest child and me—it was relaxed, easy, and congenial living. Sometimes we went out for tequila shots.

In 1990, Sappho was fourteen—a ripe old age for a Siberian Husky. She began to fail rapidly. We decided it was time and arranged to have the vet and an assistant come to the house to put her down. The four of us, John, Kathryn, Aaron and I, were there in the dining room where Sappho liked to sleep on the Oriental rug. We were all overcome with sadness. Kathryn became so agitated that our compassionate vet offered to leave and come back another time. Kathryn, still in tears, said no, it was the right time. Sappho was injected and immediately stopped breathing. Our puppy was dead.

Was I sorry we bought our puppy mill dog? We wouldn't have traded her for anything. Would I do it again?

Never.

JENNIFER J. FRANCHERE

So We Bought a Vineyard...

I remember the day I brought my husband and daughters to the property. I had seen it two days before, walked through the halls of the centuries-old house, stepped through the wet, deep grass among the vines. On a glance back toward the house from the field, a doe stepped across the path, looking convinced the place was hers alone.

Seeing it through the eyes of my husband, there was work to be done from every angle. Seeing it through the eyes of my daughters, it was an object of adventure. They explored the nooks and crannies, the closet doors that I was frankly too scared to open. The crushed stone cellar, barely tall enough to stand in. They pushed back cobwebs with barely an "Eww!" Look around this corner, that corner! Can we run in the field? Yes, of course!

Amy declared, "I know what I'm writing about when I do my weekend news at school!"

Young Erin picked me a handful of wildflowers, as she always does. I pressed them into a book, accidentally titled "The Secrets of Successful People."

We walked the lower vineyard, the pavilion, the upper vineyard, searching for signs of life among the grape plants, attempting to separate them from the tricky weeds that jumped from their roots. They struggled, some alive, some not. Some trying. I felt an ache for the woman who planted them twenty years earlier, that her work was not continued, that her efforts might all have been for naught. Or not.

Mike spoke the words that I will always remember. "You know, I can see us coming back here in two or three years, after seeing it now. It would be all fixed up, beautiful and amazing and we would say, 'Wow, can you believe that people came in and actually did this, created this?' Are we those people? *Could* we be those people?"

We are those people, and we have been those people for the past twenty years. Our daughters have grown up here, first only on weekends, then summers, then living here full time. They have lived a life of running free through fields and forest, picking wildflowers, surrounded by and immersed in nature. They have worked by our side, harvesting grapes, pruning vines, carrying supplies, stocking corks, bottles, and barrels. They have rested by our side, first in our laps, later around the fire. I believe, through us, they have seen how truly endless the possibilities are in life. That happiness isn't in a big colonial on a cul-de-sac. That a risk is worth taking, no matter the sense of it.

I remember feeling an imaginary thread pulling me forward, as it did when I left my corporate job behind the year before. I asked questions and dug through historical records to build the story of the property and its owners in my mind. Small steps at first, then bigger ones, along with the magnets of good people and good fortune that found their way to us at exactly the right time.

The same thread pulled my mother, who had faith in me.

"I haven't lived with much motivation lately, and this just feels like it might be right."

She told me she was impressed that I even looked into it, that I continued to look into it, never mind actually went through with it. And, if not for her, we couldn't have. She supported the business almost entirely in the early days while the girls were still in school. The bed and breakfast was her creation. She furnished it, decorated it, made it her own. She became our innkeeper, and gave all the guests and visitors the same treatment she gave to our relatives who visited us when I was young. The fine china and Fostoria crystal that we'd shipped around the country and back finally found a purpose.

My husband, my loving, wonderful, supportive husband, never said I was crazy, never questioned the why, only the how. He kept us alive, clothed, and fed through all those first years, making it feel like less of a risk than it really was. Giving me the space to dream, the muscle to build, and the hand to hold at the end of the day as we sat by the fire, drinking a glass of *our* wine and listening to the birds and frogs in the marshy pond beyond the lawn.

As with everything in life, the vineyard had its challenges, and we did too. Moments of "what were we thinking?" Trips we couldn't take, plans we couldn't make, our fortune tied to the Earth and whatever Mother Nature delivered. But it was enough. Enough to do the things we really wanted, enough to get our girls through college, enough for a comfortable retirement together watching others take the reins while we finally rested. Even though it was the hardest work of our lives, most days it didn't feel like work at all. We created something with meaning and merit, offering a tangible substance to gift to others, providing them an escape from the busyness of their lives.

Amy will be married here next week, as Erin was two years ago. Despite all the weddings we've held here for others, we weren't prepared for the beauty and amazement of watching our own little girl seal her love here, among the same wildflowers she once picked with her tiny hands. Now, as the girls move into the prime of their lives, and we move into the twilight of ours, we can sit back and admire the world we've created for ourselves.

Cheers.

MICHAEL J. GORDON

A Spiritual Man

It's gone now, the old, decrepit two-family Victorian house. The Thamesbridge Building Inspector had ordered the empty structure torn down before it collapsed on its own, before winter squatters could break in, build a fire in an empty room, and wind up incinerating the whole building—hopefully, with themselves not in it.

The house was one in a line of about a dozen across River Avenue from a long, Civil War era mill building that blocked all views of the water from which the thoroughfare took its name. People who glanced at its now-empty lot, however, were treated to a curious spectacle. In what had been the back yard, on a steep slope rising upwards, was a mass of over fifty old-fashioned bathtubs, set on end into the ground. Save for one at the top, which was painted red, each was painted blue inside. A stranger might have wondered what had been there, and why.

The house had belonged to Aldo Francini, a life-long resident of the town, and the first in his family to have been born in America. He had bought the home with a G.I. mortgage following his discharge from the Army after World War II. The veteran had gone to work for the State Highway Department, where he became a valued employee. Whenever people drove by a road crew, and commented on how one guy seemed to be doing all the work while five others leaned on their shovels, he was the one working.

Aldo lived in the house through summer heat, winter snows, and two wives. One-and-a-half wives, in a way. His first wife tragically passed away during a rubella epidemic only a few months after their marriage. The second—the "half"—simply left. Their union had produced no children, so neither one bothered filing for divorce—it wasn't worth the trouble, and besides, they were both Roman Catholic and the Church didn't allow it. They briefly considered asking for an annulment, but after a dozen years of marriage both of them thought that was just plain stupid, and would probably cost a lot, too. So, Aldo's wife simply moved out. He knew where she went once, but had forgotten over the years, and they never saw each other again.

As a child, Aldo had been an altar boy, and even dreamt of one day studying for the priesthood. However, as with most boys who entertain that idea, it went by the wayside as soon as he discovered girls. Still, he regularly went to confession, and to Mass every Sunday.

In his twenties, Aldo's faith was tested when his best friend since kindergarten, Barney Kaplan, asked him to be best man at his wedding. Aldo was honored, but when he casually mentioned it to the rector at St. Anthony's, the old priest became agitated. He could attend the wedding, the cleric said, but the Church absolutely forbade him to participate as best man. Since Barney was Jewish, standing up for him at the wedding would be taking part in a non-Catholic religious ceremony, a mortal sin against God.

Aldo couldn't understand why being in an old friend's wedding party was forbidden, especially since it would be in a ceremony of Jesus' own religion, for crying out loud. Besides, he was only going to stand by his friend's side, hand him the ring, and deliver a toast at dinner.

So he went ahead and served as Barney's best man, and shortly afterward left St. Anthony's and its letter-of-Canon-Law priest for the Church of St. Mary Magdalene four blocks away. The pastor there was younger, and, Aldo hoped, less doctrinaire. He remained best friends with Barney, and decided he had room in his heart for anyone who believed in God, however they practiced it.

Years passed, and on the day he turned sixty, Aldo awoke with a vision. He would build a shrine with his own hands, in his own backyard. It wouldn't honor any particular saint, but rather be an expression of his own deep spirituality. It would be open to everyone. The more he thought about it, the more convinced he became that the shrine was his true calling.

With his first wife long dead, and the second long gone, Aldo had no one around to complain that he was wasting his time and money. He was free to do as he wished, and he did.

His first step was making a deal with Nicola's Wholesale Plumbing Supply in one of the former mill buildings across the street. The wholesaler let plumbers drop off used cast iron fixtures (which it then sold by the ton to a local scrap metal dealer), and thus had a steady supply of old-fashioned, white porcelain tubs. Paying Nicola's a buck apiece, Aldo used them to create an array of niches in his backyard. He planned for one to feature a statue of Jesus, another the Virgin Mary, and the rest as many other saints as would fit in his plot of earth.

There was one problem. His backyard went nearly straight up. Not a cliff, exactly, but steep enough to be extremely difficult for most people to climb. How could visitors approach the statues?

His solution was to build two flights of steps into the hill, one on either side of the yard. He nailed together wooden forms, and filled them with concrete from an old, hand-cranked mixer he bought for twenty-five dollars. It was slow going, since each load from the mixer was enough for only a single step, and each needed days to cure before he could pour the next.

Doggedly, he kept at it every day after work, and every weekend, too. Every fourth step he hauled the mixer up with a block and tackle to pour four more. When he had completed eleven steps on each side of the yard, he poured landings on the twelfth, and connected them across with a narrow walkway.

Hauling fifty-pound sacks of ready-mix concrete on his over

sixty-year-old shoulders, he repeated the process until each side of the yard had three flights of stairs, and three landings with walkways crossing to the other side.

Next, Aldo carried each bathtub up the hill, using the block and tackle when his back hurt—which was increasingly often. Setting them on end in shallow pits, he anchored them in place by backfilling with the excavated dirt. He painted their insides a bright blue, leaving the porcelain-covered, arched rims white. Altogether, he was able to fit fifty-eight tub niches on the hillside. Fifty-seven held statues of saints, all different. The fifty-eighth, whose inside he painted red, held an icon of Jesus.

So absorbed had Aldo been in his project that it came as a complete surprise when, two weeks before his sixty-fifth birthday, he received a registered letter from the State Highway Department informing him that he was about to reach mandatory retirement age and would be out of a job. He didn't mind. His state pension, together with a small one from the military, would be sufficient to live on. And he'd be able to work on the shrine full time.

Two years later, his work was complete. The final day happened to be the Fourth of July, and in honor of that date he decided on two last minute changes, swapping out a couple of minor saints for busts of George Washington and Abraham Lincoln.

The shrine had taken him seven years of backbreaking labor, but Aldo was happy. His nearly thirty-foot high expression of spiritual feeling was complete. Now, wanting to share it with others, he hung a six-foot long, hand-painted sign on the stone wall in front of his house. It read:

HAVEN OF HOPE & TRANQUILITY

A few people driving by stopped and looked out of their car windows, or stood on the sidewalk and gawked; but they had no idea of what, exactly, the sign meant. So Aldo hung another sign below the first:

ALL WELCOME - ENTER HERE - NO CHARGE

Hesitantly at first, the curious came in. It was just a trickle—in truth, even at its peak, attendance was never all that much—but those who walked in were first startled, then charmed, by what they saw.

On each step, carved by Aldo's hand into the concrete when it was still wet, was a line or two from the Bible, set off by tiny shards of brightly-colored glass and glittering ceramics. The first flight running up the right side of the yard had verses from the Old Testament, the one on the left from the New. The next two flights on each side had quotes, which, read in sequence, constituted complete psalms. On the landings were proverbs surrounded by more eye-catching colored objects stuck into the concrete. The walkways connecting the landings were set with small pieces of tile and pottery spelling out lines from the Song of Songs. Vases and urns, some with plastic flowers, bordered them.

Adjacent to every stairway and walkway, up, down, and across, were the blue niches with white statues, plus the red one with Jesus at the top. At strategic places along the way, Aldo had placed benches so people could rest, or pray, or just take it all in.

Over the next few years, the shrine builder became a minor local celebrity. The Patriot-Gazette newspaper sent a reporter to interview him, and two college students taking a film class made a short movie about his project—but with that, his fling with fame was over.

Shortly after the shrine was finished, Aldo acquired a live-in lady friend, named Rose. He wasn't sure how it happened, but one day she was there, cooking supper, and watching television with him while they ate from folding TV trays. Now that he'd just had his seventy-fifth birthday (or maybe his seventy-sixth, he'd check his driver's license sometime to be sure) he suspected that she'd hung around because he didn't ask her for rent, and maybe she hoped he'd leave the property to her when he died—which he might, because he had no one else to leave it to, except maybe the Church of St. Mary Magdalene.

When Aldo ran short from time to time, his old friend Barney Kaplan helped him out, never asking to be repaid. Aldo felt obligated, however, so when his chum's single-story warehouse next to the mill building across the street needed a new roof, he volunteered to do the work free as a gesture of thanks. All Barney had to do was to pay for the materials, which he did.

In this way, Aldo Francini spent his later years: doing odd jobs, going to church, tending the Haven of Hope & Tranquility, napping, watching television, and warning Rose to stop bothering him about his will.

A few years later, Aldo saw his pal Barney's obituary in the Patriot-Gazette. It said he had been predeceased by his wife only a couple of months before. Aldo hadn't seen that one in the paper, and hoped Barney wasn't upset that he hadn't sent his condolences to his friend's new home in a retirement community down south.

Now in his mid-eighties, he began to find physical activity increasingly difficult, until one day he could barely walk, and was forced to move into a nursing home. Although his instinct was to fight it, Aldo realized it was time. As it was, he could barely make it up the seven steps from the sidewalk to his front door, and Rose was no help whatsoever. And so the architect and builder of the Haven of Hope & Tranquility lived in the nursing home until he passed away in his sleep, two days before his ninety-fifth birthday. A small, plain stone marked his grave in the Cemetery of St. Mary Magdalene. It gave his name, the years of his birth and death, and a simple statement: "A Spiritual Man."

As it turned out, Rose's nagging had been in vain. She did not receive the house at his passing. Nor did the Church of St. Mary Magdalene, for that matter. In fact, Aldo had left no will, and in the absence of any living relative, the eight hundred twelve dollars and forty-six cents left in his checking account was claimed by the State.

He had also died owing the town over ten years of back real

estate taxes, since once Aldo had moved into the nursing home, Rose had thrown away any mail that looked like a bill. That the delinquency was never noticed was thanks to the incompetence of the Thamesbridge Tax Collector, until one year he finally noticed the word "Deceased" stamped on the returned mail. Too lazy to do it himself, he asked the Building Inspector to go to the address and check it out.

Rose, of course, had done nothing to maintain the property. The Building Inspector promptly judged it beyond repair, and ordered it condemned and razed to the ground.

While the demolition authorization documents crept their torpid way from one bureaucrat to another, Rose convinced the Welfare Department that it should provide a home for her, claiming that she was penniless despite receiving a Social Security check every month.

All was finally ready when a Thamesbridge alderman reasoned that the town might recoup a little extra money by auctioning off the minor celebrity's niches, statues, and urns before tearing the house down and trying to sell the land.

A date for the auction was set, and the event advertised in the Patriot-Gazette.

Based on the auction turnout, Aldo Francini was more popular in death than in life. Several hundred curious people attended. The statues mostly sold for between ten and twenty dollars each, except for Abraham Lincoln, who topped the list at forty-one-fifty. The tubs were included, but no one bothered trying to remove them. The most expensive item was the Haven of Hope & Tranquility sign, which was purchased for seventy-seven dollars by one of the two former movie makers to give to the other as a wedding present. There is no record of what the recipient's new wife thought of the gift.

The next day, a bulldozer, excavator, and front-end loader, each emblazoned with the name and seal of the Town of Thamesbridge, knocked the house down. The day after that, a small parade of dump trucks carted its remains to the town landfill.

It had been only three days for the Haven of Hope & Tranquility to disappear, and the white Victorian house with it.

The town advertised the empty lot for sale, but the neighborhood had deteriorated so much that no offers were received. With no buyer, the town let it go to seed. The Tax Collector said he'd to try to sell it again the following year, but he was voted out of office and the new holder of the job couldn't be bothered. Nature took over, and the lot which had once been home to the Haven of Hope & Tranquility became overgrown with thick brush and trees.

Years before, on his way to pick up the materials to redo Barney's warehouse roof, Aldo had made a small detour into the Church of St. Mary Magdalene. A young priest who noticed him kneeling in a pew thought it odd that, as the old man got up to leave, he gave what for all the world looked like a conspiratorial wink to the statue of the parish's eponymous saint.

When the roofing job was finished, Aldo admired his handiwork from the upstairs front windows of his house across the street. He invited Barney over to see it as well. His friend took one look, clapped Aldo on the shoulder, and laughingly said, "As long as it doesn't leak."

Now, with the house gone, anyone with the fortitude to fight through the heavy vegetation, and climb past the empty niches up to the very top of the concrete steps with the Biblical verses, can look across the street and see what Barney Kaplan saw. Aldo had covered the roof of the old warehouse in perfectly laid, jet black roofing—except for where, in brilliant white, he had shingled in the shape of a giant cross.

Requiescat in pace.

JUDITH M. COOKE

A Perfectly Good Saturday Wasted

I don't know which was worse, the smell of the food or the smell of the people. I was so glad when that huge pan of tuna noodle casserole was gone, but they just brought out another vat of stinky slop for me to serve. By the way, ice cream scoops are meant to serve ice cream, and any fish that comes out of a can is cat food, no matter what the label says. But the people coming through the line didn't seem to mind. Some of them even asked for an extra plate! Of tuna noodle slop with a side of green beans! Did I mention the smell? Matt, who runs the soup kitchen, said it was "strictly one to a customer," but I gave them more if they wanted it, anything to get it done faster.

It was a freak show in there. One man had an eye swollen shut with yellow goo oozing out. Another came in wearing a tee-shirt that read "Give Blood—Play Hockey" along with pin-striped suit pants that looked like they had been driven over by a truck. And I'm pretty sure that one woman who came through the line was really a man in a dress.

"Thank you, Missy," some old lady said when I handed her a plate.

"My name isn't Missy," I said. "It's Allie."

"Okay then, Allie it is," she said, pulling along a little boy by the wrist. I didn't know that children ever came to a place like that. Some of them would have been cute if anyone dressed them right.

When the people had all come through the line, Mom came over to my station, just to rub it in I bet. "It's a whole different world in here, isn't it?" she said.

"I'll say," I grumbled.

"I'm glad you got to see how some people have to live," she preached. "There are a lot of people in this world who have it really rough."

"Yeah," I said. Sometimes the fastest way to end one of her sermons was just to agree.

Matt came out of the kitchen. "Okay folks," he said to us. "Now that the lunch rush is over, I need you all in the kitchen for clean up." Clean up? Clean up?!?

And to think I had to give up a Saturday for this!

Mom acts like she never did anything wrong in her whole life, but I know better. Nana says all the time that she never had a moment's peace with her. What a hypocrite Mom is! It wasn't like I was even breaking the law. All I did was climb out my window to meet Jackie in the park. So what if it was two a.m.? The cops who drove us home didn't even press charges, but you'd think I'd murdered someone by the way Mom and Dad yelled.

"What were you thinking?"

"Do you know how dangerous that was?"

"We didn't raise you to be a juvenile delinquent."

And because I have "too much free time on my hands," they said, the "suitable punishment" they said, was "a hard days' work where I'd see how good my life really is" they said.

On the car ride home from a perfectly good Saturday wasted, Mom said, "Life is not really fair to everyone, is it?"

"You can say that again," I answered.

KENT JARRELL

New Zealand, Elton John, and Me

A MEMOIR

In February 1990, I stood outside the offices of the Commissioner of Major League Baseball on Park Avenue in New York City. I was part of a gaggle of other reporters, working a story on the looming lockout threatening the upcoming season. It was a solid, high profile assignment, but my suddenly buzzing beeper interrupted. Instead, I was to be dispatched halfway around the world to New Zealand on an even bigger, more exotic case, one of kidnapping and child molestation. I had no way of knowing the journey would lead me to a public calling out by Elton John, the threat of jail time, and a visit to a nudist camp on the Tasman Sea.

First, I had to correctly answer three rapid fire questions when I called into the assignment desk:

1. Did I have enough material to immediately file a story on the lockout?

2. Did I have my passport?

3. Could I make it to Newark Airport in the next hour and a half?

Yes, yes, and yes, and I was on my way.

I told the news desk to book me business class to New Zealand. However, on my arrival at the airline premium check-in counter at Newark, I was informed my reservation was in coach. That was changed in an instant with my credit card, followed by a quick call back to the news desk.

"Who the hell downgraded me? For that, you will pay first class."

At which point, I hung up and ran for the gate.

Everything was fine from Newark to Los Angeles, where I picked up the connecting flight to New Zealand. As I sat down, a man across the aisle said, "I know you."

I politely answered, "Yes, thanks for saying hello. Nice to see you," which was my usual response to strangers thinking they actually knew me, instead of a vague recognition of my face from television.

The man persisted, "No, I'm Eric Foretich. I'm on the way to Christchurch to get my daughter."

Got it. Dr. Eric Foretich, the oral surgeon from northern Virginia who was hurdling across time zones to get to New Zealand to try to regain custody of his seven-year-old daughter, Hilary, and bring her back to the United States. The child was at the center of an international custody battle between her mother, Dr. Elizabeth Morgan, a plastic surgeon, and Foretich. Morgan had spent 25 months in the Washington, D.C., lockup for refusing to tell a judge Hilary's location after claiming Foretich sexually abused their child. Morgan said these events occurred during Hillary's unsupervised visits with Foretich following their divorce.

Hilary had been living in Christchurch with Morgan's parents for two years. When Foretich found out the grandparents had petitioned the courts to keep Hilary in New Zealand, he was on his way. As were reporters from all over the world. Including me, sitting next to one of the leading players, for a twelve-hour flight at thirty-five thousand feet.

After dinner, and a couple of drinks, I struck up a conversation with Foretich. He asked what I knew about what was happening in New Zealand, and how I was going to report the story. He began to talk about himself, vehement in his denial of the sexual abuse allegations, and firm in his expressions of love for his daughter.

He became guarded in his answers to my increasingly specific questions. Somewhere over the South Pacific, we ended our conversation and retreated to on and off slumber as we headed on our southeasterly flight path to New Zealand.

As we stood waiting to disembark, we said our good-byes. I walked into the terminal behind him as we approached a swarm of reporters tipped off about the doctor's arrival.

Foretich swept by the stakeout and gestured back towards me. The reporters immediately turned their attention to me and began shouting. That was a turnabout. I was used to being on the other side, shouting the questions, not caught on the receiving end in the glare of the bright lights. Now, I was the center of attention. Cameras, boom microphones, and frantic reporters all pointed at me. I liked it.

I stopped, tried to appear modest, and explained that I was simply a reporter who had talked to Foretich on the flight over. That sparked a high decibel, insistent chorus of "What did he say?

So, I pulled out my notes and did the best I could from my scribbles, scrambled time zones, lack of sleep, and the free and plentiful onboard drinks, to tell what I knew. I was aware from the size of the assembled media that my picture and voice were about to be instantly transmitted everywhere. That was just fine with me.

After about ten minutes of jabbering, I said, "Thanks everyone, gotta go."

That got me out of the terminal and right into the arms of a correspondent for TVNZ, the government-owned broadcast network. "We've been waiting for you. The car is over here. Need to move right along, you're lead interview on our late-night broadcast," he said.

"Sure," I answered. I knew that my U.S. bosses had been making arrangements to get my stories back home, and TVNZ was now my new best friend.

"Nice show back there, mate," the correspondent said. "But we will want more on our broadcast."

"Of course," I said as we proceeded to the Foreign

Correspondents Club. I mentioned what I really needed was a meal, because I was short on sleep, and wanted to make sure I was prepared for a live broadcast still a few hours away.

"No problem, but first let's show you around and make some introductions," the correspondent said as he placed a brimming pint of lager into my hands.

It was hail-fellow-well-met and the rest of the hoopla for me, the visiting fireman with the latest scoop. But there was no food in sight. Finally, I pleaded for a meal.

The gathered journalists all gave out a hearty laugh and one replied, "Oh yes, but first we have to decide when to make the switch from beer to whiskey."

"Of course," I said, acquiescing to what was obviously a local custom, which seemed to make sense to my now increasingly addled mind.

At some point after the move to whiskey, and I think not a lot of food, it was off to the studio, with my newest buddies all raising their glasses in farewell and good luck.

After a quick once-over by the makeup artist, it was into the studio. Boom. I was on the air, introduced live across New Zealand, as "our special guest, the American correspondent who flew through the night with Dr. Eric Foretich to bring us exclusive inside details of this breaking story."

Adrenaline kicked in, washing away the alcohol and exhaustion. I recounted what I knew, speaking rapidly, and punching my adjectives as I added as much drama to the story as I could. All too quickly, at least to me, my segment was over. I headed off, alone, to my hotel.

After the flurry and headlines of Foretich's arrival in New Zealand, there was a noticeable lull in the development of new angles. Foretich had dropped out of sight, trying to arrange a visit with this daughter, and privately talking with his lawyers.

I scrambled around Christchurch, sometimes with a TVNZ cameraman in tow, sometimes on my own, trying to pull together enough material to create stories to be fed back to the

U.S. It was a big cat and mouse game. I was caught up in what became the mindless excitement of the chase. The elements included staking out the well-manicured campus of Selwyn House (where Hilary attended private school), running after cars, racing around various neighborhoods, and trying to find Hilary, her mother, her father, her grandparents, or anyone who know anything about the story.

Finally, a trolling cameraman captured the prize: video of Hilary rushing from a car towards her apartment. It was pitiful. A seven-year-old girl, scurrying to safety, with a look of surprise and fear, chased down by a camera crew. I didn't shoot the tape, but I had access to it. To me, the father of a young daughter, the video was despicable—but I didn't hesitate, and immediately used it as the key ingredient of a story that I knew would get me on the air again. The producers back home jumped, and ordered four reports that would roll out through the next day's news cycle. I was back in business.

I was often recognized because of my late-night TVNZ appearance. Perceived as a leader of the pack, other reporters kept pestering me for information. Increasingly, the now large and unruly pack of international media, sometimes falling over each other, created a new story angle.

Washington Post Pulitzer Prize-winning correspondent Barton Gellman filed a report on the unfolding spectacle of an unprecedented intrusion of family privacy, headlined "New Zealand-the Media Madness."

A retired judge described the media's performance as "sickening." A deputy mayor said it was "terrible." A child psychiatrist pronounced it "outrageous." Parents of children at Hilary's school shouted "ghouls" and "vultures" at reporters.

My contribution to Gellman's story was my ranking of the media behavior as "minor league." Gellman added my colloquial language to give a little color to his story.

"Lemme tell ya, if this was anywhere in the U.S., there would be 50 camera crews, there would be satellite trucks, and they would be followed 24 hours a day," was the quote from me.

Principal Family Court Judge Patrick Mahony was particularly incensed and called reporters to a news conference. We all dutifully showed up and listened to a stern warning that the New Zealand Guardianship Act of 1968 gave him the power to "detain" us (a polite description of throwing us in jail) for contempt for publishing, without permission, any information from family court.

"The family court in this country is not open to the public. There are clear restrictions on what may be published about a case, and there are criminal penalties for those who ignore them," Mahoney said in a quote given to United Press International.

Reporters, on the defensive, and starved for any comment from an official, fired back with volleys of tough questions. Finally, the judge gave up and was chased out of his own press conference.

The prominent New Zealand law firm of Macalister Mazengarb stated the Judge's secrecy provisions applied only to the New Zealand media and that foreign reporters could report the case overseas as long as they were careful that their stories did not leak back to New Zealand.

In my own rush to judgment, I bragged to UPI that I would ignore the judge's warning, "I'm going to continue to publish and transmit to my own country what I find out in this country."

I, of course, had already reported directly to the New Zealand audience through TVNZ domestic broadcasts.

Still, underneath my bravado defense of my behavior, and often stated commitment to the journalist's creed of "the public's right to know," I felt a sense of discomfort at the blundering intrusiveness of my work on the lives of people unaccustomed to the coarseness of tabloid reporting. This was not a new feeling for me. As I strayed further from reporting on government, politics, and Washington policy in the pursuit of sensational stories that producers increasingly demanded, a darker undertow of self-doubt became an unwelcome companion to my work.

On the night of February 28th, I was completing a late-night feed back to the U.S. from a TVNZ control room when one of the studio technicians tapped me on the shoulder. Pointing to one of the monitors, he said, "Elton John just nicked you."

I said, "Who, what?"

Turning to the bank of video monitors, I saw the "Rocket Man" himself, coming in on a live feed from his concert at Addington Showgrounds, a rugby stadium in Christchurch.

Halfway through his playlist for that night, in the introduction to "Candle in the Wind," his ode to Marilyn Monroe's short, tragic, and eventful life, Elton John dedicated the song to the "little girl in Christchurch" who was being hounded and harassed by the media and, especially, by an American reporter who kept pushing the story on television. The crowd roared in approval. Cigarette lighters started flickering across the grandstands and the playing field in front of the raised stage.

That was a bit jarring. Superstar Elton John taking notice of me. I didn't have time to think about that. I was forced, instead, to concentrate on the far more immediate issue of the satellite feed of my story to the U.S. A transmission spanning the equator was always tricky. Everything had to be coordinated to the second, or your base could miss the feed entirely. In those days, satellite time was expensive, and I was only able to get tight five minute windows.

I asked the technician in a demanding tone, "Are you sure the connection is getting through the hop across the Pacific?"

The technician, glancing only quickly at my feed, and then returning to the Elton John sing-along, replied, "No problem, your spot looks good going out of here."

After a week or so, the story of Hilary and her warring parents began to get stale. No new developments appeared that could create a headline and allow me to string together a story that could be packaged and bounced around the world.

My TV bosses suggested taking a couple of days off. I pulled out a map of New Zealand's south island and zeroed in on the

Tasman Sea, 250 miles north of Christchurch. After making arrangements to rent a car the next day, I ran into a fellow reporter from the states and asked her if she wanted to come along. At that time, I was separated. Not officially divorced, but I considered myself fancy free. She was interested but said she would get back to me that evening.

Several hours later, she explained her complication. She worked for NBC and the network told her she might be able to do a story for airing on the Today Show. That would have been a big career boost for her. She was undecided whether to go away with me for a long weekend or stay put and wait for a possible shot on the highly-rated network morning show.

I understood and said, "Tell you what. See if you get anything solid in the morning. If you don't, call me and I can pick you up."

There was no phone call the next morning, so off I went. A half hour outside Christchurch, I found myself barreling along Route One, which runs up along the eastern coast. It quickly became a solitary journey on the rarely traveled two lane road, with waves pounding in from the Pacific off to my right.

Several hours later, I ended up in Nelson, a small city surrounded by mountains on three sides facing Tasman Bay. Being in the southern hemisphere, February was mid-summer and Nelson had the reputation of having one of the sunniest climates in the country.

It had been a long drive. I was tired as I stopped to ask directions to the Mapua Leisure Park. The resort's advertised claim of having "a warm community atmosphere, where peace and tranquility are legend" had attracted me. I had been able to arrange a reservation from Christchurch even in this, the high season.

Checking in at the welcoming center, I was shown to a small bungalow. After unpacking, I mixed myself a gin and tonic, and sat on the porch overlooking a dirt road leading to the beach. Almost immediately, a middle-aged couple walked into view, apparently coming back from an early evening stroll. They didn't have on a stitch of clothing.

As they approached, they gave me a friendly wave, and continued on their way.

I paused, took a hefty gulp of my drink, walked back inside, and rang up the welcoming center. The receptionist answered, "Good day, Mr. Jarrell. How are the accommodations? Everything to your satisfaction?"

"Oh yes," I said. "Everything's fine. I do have one question. I notice that the guests are not wearing clothes."

The receptionist chuckled, "Well, we are clothing optional. Didn't they tell you that when you booked in Christchurch?"

"Well, no. But that's no problem. Can you do me a favor? Can you place a collect call for me to the United States?" I said as I recited the number for the news desk in Washington.

The call came through a few minutes later. The desk manager back in D.C. said, "Kent. Where the hell are you? We weren't expecting to hear from you for a couple of days."

"I'm in a nudist camp. This will be on my expense report because this is on you. I'll call back in a few days. You can reach me at this number in an emergency but for now, I'm taking off my clothes and mixing myself another gin drink."

As I was hanging up, I heard the desk manager yell out to the rest of the newsroom, "Jarrell's gone native. He's in a nudist camp, drinking, and he's thrown away his clothes."

For the next two days, I adjusted to my new environment, a simple task for a reporter used to seamlessly changing behavior and opinion like a chameleon. I shed clothes for the walk to the beach, wore just sneakers for a hike, donned a swimsuit when I was in the water (the notorious sharks of the South Pacific), and, for the sake of decorum, dressed up in shorts for dining.

Along the way, I learned the rule of conversation in a clothes optional setting: eye to eye contact, no looking down, and light and easy talk in the bright sun with no cover.

I was recognized from my television reports. One of the tricks of fame, both large, and in my case, small, is that people you don't know, but who know of you, don't always come right out and pepper you with criticism.

The casual acquaintance often prefers to bask in the reflected warmth and perceived glow from the presence of a luminary by glossing over the uncomfortable. The banter centered on my visit to New Zealand, the beautiful weather, and my single status at the resort. Having been stood up by a "lady friend" reporter for my weekend excursion was found to be quite humorous.

My trip to New Zealand ended not with a bang, but with the deflating whimper of stories failing to get on the air. Finally, after two and a half weeks, I found myself hurtling back across the international dateline, heading home, with another notch on my reporter's belt.

Many years later, I tripped across a retrospective story in LA Weekly. Dr. Foretich never got custody and went back to his dental practice in Virginia. Hilary moved to Los Angeles, sharing an apartment with her mother overlooking the sheen and promise of Beverly Hills. An aspiring musician in her twenties, Hilary changed her name to Elena Mitrano. "Voiceless", her YouTube music video, describes "endless seas of tragedy, too many to speak of."

I wonder which wave in those seas was me.

JUDITH BANNON SNOW

Back Story

After reading my MRI, my capable, compassionate, and conservative back doctor gave me the news:

"I'm sorry. If I were you, I would have back surgery."

"What? I've had a bad back my whole life. I've vowed never to have an operation on my back."

"You have two options," she said. "You can have an operation or you can spend the rest of your life in a wheelchair."

I never thought an MRI could make my cry, but this one did.

The MRI showed my two lowest lumbar vertebrae displaced by half an inch—L4 in front and L5 in back. My spinal cord was squished between these two vertebrae. It looked awful.

Next step: find a surgeon, ASAP. "You want a neurosurgeon that specializes in backs. They are the plumbers—they care about the nerves," said Dr. Kathryn Barnard. "The orthopedic surgeons are the carpenters—they care about the bones."

I made an appointment with the 'best' back surgeon in New Mexico. "A lot of people don't like me," he said.

Neither did I, although it wasn't his manner that put me off. It was that he didn't know what he was talking about, promising to perform surgical interventions he had never tried. Scary.

Richard, my husband, bought me two "Top Docs" books that included top doctors across the nation in all specialties. As I pored over the books, I found very few neurosurgeons who specialized in spines. Apparently, most neurosurgeons were interested in brains.

Finally, I found what looked like the perfect one. Dr. John

Hsiang was a highly rated surgeon at Swedish Hospital's Neuroscience Institute in Seattle. I scheduled a consultation for mid-October.

A month before, my first husband John and his third wife Nancy, who were touring the Southwest, stayed with us in our old double-adobe home just north of Santa Fe. After a good two-day visit, they said as they were leaving, "Let us know if you ever need anything. Anything at all."

I dialed their number in Seattle.

"Hi John, hi Nancy. I have a consultation with a back surgeon in Seattle. Can Richard and I stay with you?"

"Of course," said Nancy. "You're family."

On Thursday, October 11, 2007, we met Dr. Hsiang and his physician's assistant, Linda Lao. They had a leather sofa in the consultation room and served us orange juice. We liked them and the ambiance. We decided to schedule the surgery.

Dr. Hsiang looked at his schedule and said, "How about the sixteenth?"

"The sixteenth of what?"

"October."

"But that's next Tuesday!"

"I have a cancellation."

Richard and I looked at each other. "We'll take it."

We lived it up with John and Nancy until Monday evening.

The Neuroscience Institute was in a refurbished hospital, with old patient rooms where spouses could stay during surgery and recovery. Richard would be staying only a few hundred feet from my room.

As I prepped for the next morning's surgery, I panicked.

"I can't do this. I want to leave. I want to go home right now!"

"You can't leave," said Richard. "Anyway, you have to do it sooner or later."

"What if I die on the table?"

"You won't. Trust me."

My admission was early the next morning. After going over my history and medications with three different nurses, I met with my anesthesiologist.

"I have a question."

"About what?" he said.

"Lethal injections."

"Wow. Nobody has ever asked me that."

"How is it that you can put a dog to sleep instantaneously with no pain whatsoever, while lethal injections take minutes and hours of agony and sometimes fail?"

"All members of the American Society of Anesthesiologists take an oath to have absolutely nothing to do with lethal injections."

"Well," I said, "that would explain it."

Surgery over. Three or four hours after drifting off to sleep, I awoke in my room to see Richard and my brother, Phil, who lived nearby in a small houseboat in Seattle, standing across the room.

"Do you know these gentlemen?" asked the nurse.

"No, but they look like very nice men."

Nurse floored, me smirking.

"Do you know where you are?"

Although I knew very well that I was in Seattle's Swedish Neuroscience Institute, the fictitious hospital in the popular TV series *Grey's Anatomy* came to mind.

I replied, "Yes, I do. Seattle Grace!"

Nurse distressed, the three of us smirking. She didn't get the joke.

I was on a morphone (similar to morphine) drip. I had a button to push more sedative into my IV.

I said, "Less email, more phone."

Nurse leaves. We laugh. It hurts!

The hospital staff brings me inedible food. The nurses make me eat it. I throw up. The nurses give me anti-nausea meds. Time passes, anti-nausea meds wear off. The hospital staff brings me inedible food. The nurses make me eat it. I throw up. The nurses give me anti-nausea meds. Time passes, anti-nausea meds wear off.

Richard suggests giving me anti-nausea meds before I eat. The nurses are insulted by this idea.

Meanwhile, I can't keep down food or water.

"You have to drink water. Your blood pressure is dangerously low—it's 65/42."

I drink water. I throw up. My blood pressure is even lower.

Although I am very scared, I think this is hilarious. The surgery went perfectly, but I am going to die of low blood pressure. Too funny!

Richard suggests increasing the saline concentration in my IV. This time, the nurses listen. My blood pressure begins to rise.

Yay! Maybe I won't die after all.

JAMES E. McKIE, JR.

Sandbox Gardeners

A MEMOIR

John and Albina Mellom, nicknamed Jack and Bina, lived in an old, two-story mill house in Oxford, Massachusetts. In 1941, the Mellom's only daughter, Irene, and her husband, Jim McKie, had blessed the Melloms with their first grandchild, Jimmie. Over the next six years, grandchildren Jackie and Rita joined the family. Unfortunately, the McKies lived in New York City, a four-hour drive away. Irene and Jim wanted their three children to grow up knowing their Mellom grandparents, and to enjoy summer escapes from the city. So it was, that Irene, Jim, Bina, and Jack hatched a plan that hopefully would benefit all. Irene and the children would spend July and August with Jack and Bina in Oxford, and Jim would join them in August when he took his annual vacation.

The summers of 1948 and 1949 showed that the vacation plan had worked out better than any of them could have imagined. The grandparents looked forward to each summer when their family escaped New York City and came to Massachusetts to enjoy the countryside with them.

In late June of 1950, Jack and Bina were anticipating the annual arrival of Irene and the grandchildren. Over the last three years, Jack and Bina had enhanced the one-acre property with lawns, shrubs, and gardens, complementing an existing stand of aromatic white pines. Both loved flowers and vegetables, and they wanted gardens that would yield a rainbow of colors and a plethora of edibles. While it would always be a work in progress, it was heaven to their visiting family, especially the grandchildren.

Jack and Bina were waiting at the bus stop on Route 12 and greeted their daughter and grandchildren when the bus arrived. A short uphill walk on Depot Road brought them to house Number 3. Nine-year-old Jimmie and seven-year-old Jackie had run ahead and frolicked with joy on the green front lawn. Three-year-old Rita had soon joined her brothers, while the adults were the last to arrive, lugging the suitcases. While the children played, Jack and Bina showed Irene the new flowerbeds and vegetable gardens they had installed. The beauty of it all took Irene aback. As a surprise for the grandchildren, Jack had made two swings by the pine trees. He had also been busy under some elms, where he had created a patio featuring a swinging sofa, folding chairs, and a large picnic table.

A few days after the grandchildren arrived, Jack asked Jimmie and Jackie if they would like to help him water the plants. Both signed up. They gave the flowers and vegetables a good dousing, and Grandpa praised them for their work. The next day, Jimmie asked if he could have his own vegetable garden, and Jackie immediately followed with the same question. Jack thought it was a great opportunity to teach them the joys of growing one's own food.

So, later that day, when his friend Fred drove up the driveway, Jack told him about the boys' interest in gardening. Fred offered to drive them to the Oxford hardware store and its nice selection of seeds. Jack and Fred showed the boys the store's large, rotating seed packet display and let them choose one each. Jimmie picked beets because he liked the purple-red color of the drawing on the packet. Jackie's favorite color was orange, so he took carrots.

Upon returning home, the boys wanted to plant their seeds right away. Grandpa took them to one of his vegetable gardens, and suggested that each boy stake out a small area in the rich, black soil. Jimmie and Jackie were not pleased—they wanted to have their own garden, not Grandpa's. Grandpa tried explaining that the soil in his garden would give the beets and carrots the best chance to grow big and become ripe. After failing to persuade them, Jack told them to pick out their own spot.

After searching and searching, the boys decided on a sandbox filled with sand that Jack planned to use to make concrete. They liked the sandbox because it was where they had spent many hours playing with their toy cars, driving and crashing them in a pretend desert. They also liked it because it was close to the tap, where Grandpa kept his large watering can. However hard he tried, Jack was not able to convince them that vegetables would not grow in sand. In the end, he gave up and instructed his grandsons to be sure to water the seeds every day.

From the kitchen window, Jack, Bina, and Irene peeked as the boys filled the watering can, carried it to the sandbox and liberally sprinkled its entire area. Jimmie then picked up a stick and drew a line that divided the wet sand area in half. He staked out the left half for himself and told Jackie to plant in the right. Meanwhile, the adult spies in the kitchen watched the entertainment.

Jimmie told Jackie that the best way to plant the seeds was to poke a line of holes in the wet sand with a finger, pour some seeds from the packet into each hole, and then fill the hole with sand. Jimmie then demonstrated the sequence for Jackie to copy. Although he had made about eight holes, Jimmie ran out of seeds after the fifth. From the kitchen window some six-feet away, it was difficult to tell how many seeds had been poured into the five holes. Before Jimmie finished his demonstration, Jackie began making a bunch of finger holes. His seed packet was empty after only four holes. Jack Mellom that each packet had held about two-dozen seeds, so a few holes got way too many seeds and the rest got none.

Turning back to the window, the grandparents and Irene continued watching as the final act was completed. Jimmie and Jackie each drove a stick into the sand in front of their plots, onto which they impaled their empty paper packets. They concluded with another full watering can's contents sprinkled over the planted areas.

Moments later, the two boys ran into the house to announce that they'd made their vegetable gardens and wanted everyone to come out and see their handiwork. With straight faces, the adults and Rita followed the boys' to their garden. Grandpa emphasized how very important it was for Jimmie and Jackie to water their gardens, twice every day that it didn't rain. Mom and Grandma poured praise on the two towheads for a job well done, while Rita now seemed to be saying that she too wanted her own garden (the adults pretended not to understand what she was saying).

Each day the boys dutifully watered their gardens, once in the morning and once in the late afternoon. This lasted for a week. During the second week, adults began to notice an occasional lapse of watering memory in the boys. By week three, Jimmie was on strike, and Jackie soon joined him. They complained that the watering can was too heavy when filled, and besides, watering was doing no good.

Early in August Daddy arrived from New York in his old, black Chevy. The children loved it when he joined them in Oxford because he would take them for drives and long walks in the countryside. One day, Dad said to the boys that a little bird had told him they were now vegetable gardeners. Was that true? If so, he wanted to see their gardens. Glumly, Jimmie told him that, yes, it was true that they had planted gardens, but they were no gardeners.

"Are you watering every day?"

"No," they replied, "because nothing was growing and it never would."

The morning after, they showed him their sad gardens, and Dad persuaded them to water once again. They did, but the looks on their young faces only signaled hopelessness.

That afternoon, Fred stopped for a visit and asked if he could take the kids out for a drive to get some ice cream. In a flash they were in his car, and off they went to the Montrose Dairy, about six miles away. Upon returning, Fred said he had to get a move on for some errands, but asked Jack to let him know how the rest of the afternoon turned out.

After Fred left, Grandpa asked the boys if they'd checked their gardens for any change. Yes, they replied—they'd looked before going for ice cream and still saw no sign of life emerging. He persuaded them to go look again because, as he put it, sometimes you have to dig a bit to see if anything is growing. Dutifully, but slowly, the two boys dragged their feet to the sandbox. Jimmie knelt down and dug where he remembered making his first hole. As he dug, all of a sudden, his hand found something round and hard. He grabbed and pulled it out—it was A LARGE RED BEET! Jackie dropped to his knees and began digging like a mole. Seconds later, he pulled out—A LONG ORANGE CARROT! The boys didn't seem to notice that no foliage was attached to either vegetable (the store clerk had removed the leaves before Bina could tell him to leave them on).

Like crazed miners striking pay dirt, the boys kept digging until they found many more beets and carrots. The four adults burst into uncontrolled laughter. Rita didn't understand why her parents and grandparents were laughing, but joined in with them anyway.

The show outside the window kept getting better and better. Jack went out to congratulate the boys, casually suggesting that they might check around in the backyard for any other vegetables or fruits that were ripe and needed to be brought into the house. Jackie immediately found a large watermelon in Grandpa's zucchini bed. Jimmie discovered some asparagus stalks that must have gotten planted by mistake next to the corn stalks. Jackie then found a whole bunch of ripe raspberries lying beneath a gooseberry bush. But when Jimmie saw a large, ripe grapefruit in the crotch of a young maple tree, the jig was up!

The boys brought their cornucopia of vegetables and fruits into the kitchen, and noticed the adults all had red eyes and tear-stained faces. All the adults except Grandma, that is. She was upstairs changing because, in recent years, she found it very difficult to laugh without tears on her face and pee in her pants.

When Jimmie and Jackie returned with their family to the big city in late August, they brought small gifts for their best friends at home, and a large gift—a colorful collection of funny stories, riddles, and jokes they learned that summer. And, the first funny story they couldn't wait to tell was how not to grow vegetables and make your elders laugh.

JUDITH M. COOKE

The Businessman

"**S**tick to the Methodists," Mom always said. "Dating a girl from another church will only lead to problems."

Was Mom ever right! My name is William Robert Hopkins. My family calls me Billy Bob, but my friends call me Bubba. I come from a long line of farmers. My dad was a farmer, and his dad, and his dad before that. But me, I am a businessman. I work at the Tiller Seed & Hardware Store behind the register, and I would like to share with you the story of how I got to be a businessman.

It all started with a woman. Her name is Lurleen, and she's the prettiest little flower I ever saw. And it's not just me that thinks so; she was named Miss Zucchini in the Harvest Festival. I'd had my eye on Lurleen for an awful long time, but I was afraid to make my move. Then I saw her one day leaving the Quick 'N Pick with a big bag, and I offered to carry it for her. It turns out the bag was real light, but she acted so grateful that I got up my courage and asked her to join me for a movie on Friday night. She said yes.

I can tell you that I was really looking forward to that date. I picked out my best shirt and shined my shoes. I even practiced my smile in the mirror to make sure I looked right. But then, when I got ready to go pick her up, the car wasn't in the yard anymore. Mom had forgotten that I was going to use it, and she up and went shopping all the way in Scotts Bluff. I was not going to miss my date with Lurleen, so I had to take the only vehicle that was left: the tractor. A year ago when the tractor seat got all wobbly, Dad replaced it with an old school bus seat; that way the dog could ride with him in the fields. I hated to put Lurleen in the dog's seat, but I didn't have a lot of choice at this time. The tractor may move slow and not be much to look at, but a ride's a ride. When I picked up Lurleen, her sister saw the tractor and started to laugh, but Lurleen was a true lady. She just climbed right up and didn't say a word.

The movie was fine, I guess. Lurleen picked it out, and she seemed to enjoy it. We shared some popcorn, and she let me hold her hand. Things were going so well that I suggested we go take a ride to the reservoir where the buttes show in the distance. She said that would be fine, so we climbed back in the tractor and headed out into the sand hills. I knew just the spot to take her, just over the hill that looks out over the water and the Miller Farm. When I parked the tractor there, Lurleen said, "This is nice." I thought that was a good sign, so I put my arm around her, and she moved closer. When I leaned in to kiss her, it felt like the earth was moving. But then I realized the earth was fine; we were moving. The tractor was sliding down the sand hill. I pulled on the tractor's emergency brake, but we just kept going. I tried to put the tractor in reverse, but the wheels only spun. You just can't get no traction on no sand hill.

As the tractor started moving faster and faster downhill, I jumped out, but Lurleen just sat there holding onto her pocketbook, and staring at the water. "Jump, Lurleen! Jump!" I yelled to her, but all she did was sit there stiff as a board, not even making the slightest peep the whole way into the water. I was pretty sure Lurleen could swim, after all she wore a bathing suit in the Harvest Festival beauty pageant, but she wasn't acting like a normal person right then. So I ran into the water to help her out. I got all wet trying to be a gentleman, but she would not even take my hand. At this time, I knew our date was over, but the tractor was pretty well covered by water and still slowly sinking, so we had to walk the four miles back to town.

The worst part though was when I had to tell my dad what

had happened. It took two neighbors and three pickup trucks to pull the tractor out of the reservoir the next day. The neighbors thought this was the funniest thing they ever saw, but I had never seen my dad so angry. When we got home, he was red and shaking and he said, "Billy Bob, you ain't cut out to be no farmer!"

And that is why I now work at the Tiller Seed and Hardware Store and have become a businessman.

ISABELLE DOUGLAS SEGGERMAN

Queen Bee and the Three-Legged Rabbit

My friend Buffy and I have known each other for about forty years. Our friendship developed when we met as divorced mothers, raising our children in suburban Washington, D.C. Our financial circumstances were quite different. She had been married to Sinclair Belmont, a scion of the famously wealthy family, for fourteen years, until he ran off with their forty-year-old nanny. During the divorce, Buffy had managed to extract two homes and more than her fair share of money. I had more or less escaped from my four-year marriage with my sanity, my daughter, and a few blankets.

She invited me to visit for a few days in Newport, Rhode Island, where she still summered in the spacious townhouse she'd kept. It sounded good, and I had never been there, so I kennelized the dogs, stopped the mail, forgot the newspapers, and the following Monday morning set off to Union Station to catch the 8:40 a.m. Amtrak to Newport. Well, almost to Newport. That city is not on a regular train line, so Buffy said that she would send her handyman to pick me up at the station in Kingston.

The train left Washington on time. I found a seat alone and settled back for the seven-hour-plus ride. I hadn't been on a train for years, and was looking forward to the ride. I'd brought my laptop and yellow legal pad, planning to catch up on some writing. However, the train's Wi-Fi did not work, and the ride wasn't smooth enough to write by hand. Conscience clear, I read the paperback novel I'd brought, dozed, and enjoyed some scenery on route.

The train arrived almost exactly on time at the small station, and a man on the platform immediately identified himself as my driver. I planned to sit in the front seat next to him, but he insisted that I sit in the back. Forty-five minutes later, my three long nights and three-and-a-half days with Buffy began.

She welcomed me to her house, which had a gorgeous view of the water. Before I could even find where my room was, she was on the phone ordering groceries to be delivered—chicken parts for our dinner the first night, more chicken parts for the guests she had invited the next night, Bibb lettuce for two dinners, a few fresh herbs, and a baguette.

"Tonight will be our catch up evening," she said.

I was directed upstairs to my room and told to settle in, nap, and meet her downstairs in the kitchen at 6:15. I wasn't tired. In fact, I felt restored after the train ride. However, there did not seem to be another option, so I assumed that I was supposed to remain in my suite until the designated hour.

My room was quite pretty. Two white, quilted twin bedspreads had the Belmont crest in the center of each. Her maiden name was James, but she preferred to use the monogram and crest of her first and only husband's family.

A vase of fresh roses sat on a bureau, the pink of the flowers matching the pink of the Belmont-monogrammed towels in the adjoining marble-tiled bathroom. A walnut veneered Louis Quatorze style writing table held a navy blue, leather-bound guest book. On the bedside table rested several of Buffy's self-published books. I decided to skip the one she had written about bad house guests, and took my relaxing novel outside to enjoy the fresh air and smell of the ocean.

Masses of floral chintz draperies concealed a sliding glass door leading to a small faux wood balcony with a cast iron settee and a small glass-topped table. The curtains did not clear the tops of their frames completely. If one were not cautious, their tops could tear upon opening. So like a little caterpillar, I moved through them and plunked myself down on the uncomfortable iron settee and read until the appointed hour to meet downstairs.

Sitting on a very small, pastel stripe covered, high stool, at her direction I helped Buffy prepare dinner by washing and tearing lettuce leaves into bite-sized pieces. She said that her mornings began with coffee upstairs in bed while she read the papers, and watched the BBC news on television. She said she would come down around 10:30, and we would do whatever she had planned for the day.

She pointed to a clear plastic tray covered by a peach-color, embroidered linen placemat with matching napkin. It was for my solo breakfast the next morning. Silverware, a coffee cup, juice glass, and small plate had been placed on it. There were four croissants in a clear box on the counter. I was told that I could have one for breakfast.

Thus would my mornings begin, collecting the tray, pouring my coffee and juice, taking my bread, and returning to my room while trying to balance the tray and not spill anything on the way. It made me nervous—her carpet was white. No accidents occurred the first two mornings.

So, upstairs and out on the Juliet balcony, without benefit of the Wall Street Journal or the Washington Post, I sat and read my paperback until our day of exploration would begin.

During our first dinner together, over glasses of a chilled, mediocre pinot grigio, my hostess described the things she had planned for my stay. I was to have an hour and a half tour of "The Breakers," the Vanderbilt mansion, the next morning, while she went to an important appointment. That evening she had invited four single ladies of a certain age to dinner. On Wednesday, we were to pick up a Belmont cousin of her ex-husband's and go to the private chapel of a close friend, Folly, to lay flowers in his memory. Then the three of us would continue on to the Newport Art Museum and a Dutch treat lunch in the museum café.

Buffy was wearing long white slacks during our first night

together. I still had on my brown linen and rayon, non-wrinkle traveling pants. She asked me what I thought of her new knee. As I could not see it, my response was, "I assume the operation was a success, because you are still walking!"

She had never been an avid athlete during all the years we had known each other, so I asked how hard her physical therapy had been afterwards.

"It wasn't painful at all. I went to this marvelous rehab place in Narragansett where all of Newport goes twice a day for three weeks. The doctor gave me a controlled substance before each session," she purred. By "all of Newport," I assumed she meant descendants of the Gilded Age crowd.

After putting the dishes in the dishwasher, and before being sent to bed, I was told that there was one more thing that needed to be done. Buffy, never known to be an animal lover, had agreed to pet sit her daughter's rabbit, a three-legged Flemish Giant named Napoleon, for a week while the daughter and son-in-law were on vacation in Florida. The bunny had been with her for two days and had not eaten, or drunk much water. Nor had he used the litter box in the master bath off Buffy's bedroom.

I was appointed to discuss the situation with the rabbit, who remained huddled under a corner of Buffy's queen-sized bed.

In order to reach the frightened, disoriented bunny, I did a belly crawl under the bed, where the two of us came to an understanding. He ate the baby carrot trail I had made for him as I shimmied backwards out from under.

It was while I was getting up from my hands and knees that I heard Buffy's blood curdling shriek. She noticed that Napoleon had indeed gone to the bathroom… on the corner of the white bedroom rug. Out came the club soda, baking soda, and a Belmont-monogramed face cloth. It was a relief for me to know that Napoleon was well enough to eat, drink, and piddle.

My hostess felt differently. Just as her attitude toward children is "to be seen and not heard," toward animals it is that they be well groomed, obedient and go to the bathroom in their assigned places. She called her vacationing daughter and left a message complaining about the utter and complete ruination the three-legged creature had caused, and then telephoned her sister, a woman who had written books about domestic animals.

Buffy's sister recommended that the rabbit be kenneled for the rest of its visit, but my (and the bunny's) hostess decided that she could endure the animal for the rest of its scheduled time with her. She felt that I was a calming influence on it, and could help her cope with the beastie until her daughter returned in a few days. She was also determined that the younger woman would replace the rug immediately upon coming home.

Tuesday morning began in a relatively mild way when I met Buffy downstairs at 10:30. Then I mentioned that a cut on my arm had opened during the night, resulting in a spot of blood the size of a dime on the top sheet. My hostess demanded that I strip the bed immediately. She would have to get me a clean sheet, and complained that her maid (who was nowhere in residence during my entire stay) had so much laundry to do as it was.

I explained that I had taken the sheet off the bed, washed the spot off completely with cold water, and that it was now drying on the shower door in my room. That pacified her for the moment.

Then she whisked me off for my tour of The Breakers while she went to her dressmaker to have a ball gown recut. Buffy met me afterward, and I treated her to lunch before we headed home for her designated nap. Then it was downstairs, exactly at 6:00 p.m. as commanded, to help prepare dinner for her four friends' scheduled 6:45 arrival. She fretted about the weather, but decided that it would be pleasant enough to eat outside.

I fetched the two card tables from her office and set them up on the porch off her living room. Then I took the stained table cloth she handed me and placed it over the tables. Fortunately, Buffy noticed the stains and told me to take one off a corner tea table in her living room and use it instead. I decided not to mention that it was stained as well, but proceeded to place the salt shakers and a vase filled with flowers over the spots.

As I set the stainless steel utensils out on the table, Buffy came over to inspect and told me that I had not done it correctly. She rearranged a bit of flatware and said, "This is how it is done in England."

I piped up, saying that her way was how it was done in good restaurants, but not in England.

Buffy said, "Each to his own."

Then she wanted me to cut the lemons paper thin for the chicken dish.

"I can't," I said. "I have arthritis in my fingers."

"You should have stem cell replacement," she advised. "Now, why don't you go up and change for dinner?"

"What's wrong with what I have on?" I asked, completely perplexed in my designer linen pants and a long sleeved shirt recently purchased from Nordstrom's.

With a royal flick of the wrist she announced, "No one wears day clothes to my dinner parties. Everyone dresses for them."

So up I went, to put on the only skirt I had brought with me, a short, navy blue cotton number with a crimson floral print from Talbot's. I combined it with a blue t-shirt with a crimson beaded neckline. Back down in the kitchen, I told her that this was as good as it was going to get.

Fortunately, my new attire was acceptable, for at 6:45 p.m. her four guests arrived exactly on time. They all wore cotton t-shirts, some long-sleeved, some short, and each—Jenny, Beth, Amelia, and Sally—were similarly clad in well-worn, pastel-colored, cotton pedal pushers. Buffy opened the presents they had brought.

Her gracious, and not unexpected, thank you was, "Oh, you shouldn't have!"

I said, "Oh, yes you should have!" Everyone laughed and thus began a very compatible and amusing evening. We discovered that Sally had come from a town where I had once lived. Jenny was creative, and a former university professor of music. Her presence was comforting.

Jenny asked, "What did you think of The Breakers?"

My response was simple: "If I knew you better, I would tell you." After a bit of coaxing and another drink, I opened up. "I felt the place had no soul. The collection of art and furniture seemed to represent a rich man's indiscriminate purchases, and outside, every tree and plant had been manipulated to fit his idea of perfection."

"You put that well," Jenny responded. "Actually, it's what I have always felt, but could not find the right words." A genuine descendant of one of the old, pre-Gilded Age Newport families saw things as I did.

The group of ladies left at the relatively appropriate hour of 9:45 p.m., and we put the dishes into the dishwasher. Once upstairs for the night, I went to check on Napoleon. Miracle of miracles, he had pooped, although he had missed the litter box by a few inches. It seemed that he was adjusting. Buffy was not amused, but did not command me to pick up the mess.

Now that I was becoming accustomed to the rhythm of Buffy's house, Wednesday began rather easily. I went downstairs at around eight, got my coffee, fruit and leftover croissant and took them back to my room. Unfortunately, I spilled the coffee on my tray carrying it upstairs. I washed the place mat, draped it over the shower door (my default drying location) and decided not to mention this mishap to my hostess. Being traumatized by the rabbit was enough, she did not need any more.

At the requested hour I went downstairs to meet Buffy for the day's planned activities. She was sitting in her office. From the little I had seen, it appeared that the space was used only to order clothing from on-line catalogues and peruse exotic travel sites for her next destination.

This day I heard the end of a phone conversation. "What do you think I am? I am not a social secretary, and I do not have time for this!" she said in a queenly voice to someone at the other end of the line. Noticing me hesitating at the open door, she explained that Jenny had just called to get my e-mail address, but that she—Buffy—was so busy with office work that she simply did not have time for this type of interruption. I wondered whether Jenny would ever be sent my address or phone number.

Before leaving the house, Buffy told me to go upstairs and bring down two of the dozen roses from my welcome bouquet (I brought three), as we would not have time to stop at the florist to get anything for the chapel. I didn't ask if I had a choice! We then left to pick up Lottie Belmont, a cousin of Buffy's former husband. Buffy gave an unabridged biography of Lottie's life on the way over, including juicy tidbits that should have been left in the family closet.

We were on our way to a small, private, stone chapel to place the roses at the foot of Folly's grave. (Folly had always been a personal favorite of Buffy's. He had been on a first name basis with many English royals, which impressed her greatly.)

"Do you realize that Folly was the only person I know who had the Queen of England make him scrambled eggs for breakfast in Buckingham Palace?" Buffy asked, showing off. I wondered how this newfound knowledge could possibly enrich my life in any way.

After entering the chapel and placing the flowers in Folly's memory at the base of a tall cross, it was off to the Newport Art Museum and lunch in its café.

Lottie ordered a grilled chicken sandwich, while Buffy and I split a roast beef wrap. I picked up a fruit-flavored bottled water drink with zero calories to go with my sandwich. It was delicious, almost making me forget the chilled white French burgundy I usually have with friends at lunch.

After eating and a tour of the place, we dropped Lottie back at her home and continued to Buffy's daughter's house for an afternoon swim. We changed in a small cabana next to the pool. I chose not to swim, but Buffy did three laps in the 82 degree water. While wrapping a large towel around herself when she got out, she announced how much she loved a good workout.

After she changed from her aubergine Olympic-style bathing suit into dry clothes, we went back to her place to ready ourselves for drinks at Sally's condo. In order to avoid embarrassing my hostess, I changed into the same damn cotton floral skirt and t-shirt that I had worn for dinner the night before.

Sally lived only a few doors away, so we walked. Wearing tan slacks and a short sleeved rose-colored blouse, she received us very graciously at her front door. Then, on her rear deck, we met her two Belmont guests. One, in his early twenties, did handyman jobs for her. The other, Pierre Belmont, was about eighty-five. He wore a navy blue blazer and a pink button down shirt open at the neck. More importantly, he had one of the kindest faces and sweetest smiles that I had encountered since my arrival in Newport.

While the younger Belmont got us our drinks, Sally took me on a tour of the first floor of her 3,500 square-foot condo. It had extremely high ceilings, which gave the space breathability. The whole place seemed to be big for a single lady, yet not cavernous. It had a cozy feeling.

The walls displayed a varied and eclectic array of paintings. Some, such as those by James Buttersworth, were quite valuable. Others, done by her grandchildren, were priceless for family only. Her "smalls" on tables and cabinet shelves ranged from 18th century Limoges boxes to sea shells from a beach in Florida. Each seemed to represent a memory for Sally. The collection gave me the feeling that she and her husband had enjoyed a very happy marriage, and that Sally had chosen to be surrounded by mementos of a good life.

Gin and tonic in hand, I went out to the deck and sat next to Pierre. We had an interesting conversation about bees and beekeeping. He had a great number of hives on his property, and by chance, I had gotten a tutorial on the subject earlier in the week from Allen, my tree man, who raised the little honey-makers as a hobby.

Pierre and I had been attentive to each other during our conversation, in fact, so much so that Buffy chose to react to it on our walk back to her place, although she had not heard a word he and I had spoken to each other.

"You know, Pierre was absolutely head over heels in love with me for years, and wanted desperately to marry me. Unfortunately, his wife was not well, so he could not leave her. And you know that I do not have affairs with married men," she stated. I hadn't known any of this, nor did I really care.

Our last night's dinner was predictable. A glass of mediocre white wine together in the kitchen while Buffy tossed some pasta in a pot, drained it, and added some olive oil and the leftover tomatoes from the salad we'd had a few nights before. We ate outside.

As we were nibbling on the back deck, Buffy mentioned an incident that happened a few months before with her former husband, Sinclair, who still lives in one of the Belmont summer places in Newport. She had bumped into him at the local market, and greeted him with, "Hello, how are you?"

His reply was a straightforward, "Do I know you?" Buffy felt strongly that he had the beginnings of Alzheimer's disease.

After rinsing the dishes and putting them in the washer, it was time for me to check on the furry, three-legged guest. He had eaten; that was a good sign. He had pooped, another good sign. That he had defecated slightly outside of his litter box—not such a good sign. I crawled under the bed where he huddled in a back corner so that we could have our good-night, sweet dreams chat.

I went to bed with my novel, even after completing it the day before. The reread was far better than one of Buffy's self-published commentaries. Buffy went back to her office to give American Express hell for not acknowledging some travel miles she believed she was owed.

Sleep came slowly for me. I kept thinking about Sally's happy marriage and Buffy's disappointing one, but mainly about what brings single women together. In Buffy's and my cases, it was the very married milieu of suburban Washington, D.C., where the wives, happily married or not, looked upon divorced women as threats. Buffy, Sally and their other Newport lady friends came together, I believe, because it is often better to be with someone rather than alone. I did not sleep well.

Early the next morning, the pattern was broken. My hostess remained in bed, and I made the coffee, hoping and praying the entire time that I had put the grounds in the correct slot and the water in its rightful place. With that accomplished, I put a cup on my plastic breakfast tray, skipped the last of the now very stale croissants, and returned to my room. I wished for the rabbit's company. Finally, tired of my confinement, I went down to the living room to read.

Buffy awoke around 10:00. She went into the kitchen, got a cup of coffee with cream and grabbed the croissant I had chosen not to eat. She marched into the living room, nibbling, spilling crumbs along the way, and announced how yummy the leftover croissant was. Then she launched into a rather uninformed political discourse about how great her preferred candidate for president was during this election year. We are not of the same parties. I remained silent. She took that as a concession and victory for her choice.

It was time to get to the station for my return trip home. Buffy wanted to get her car washed before dumping me at the station, but construction delayed the traffic along the way. This infuriated her. Fortunately, she realized that it was better to get her house guest to the train on time rather than having her car sprayed with soap suds and water.

After a quick kiss on the cheek, and a "Wasn't this a wonderful catch-up?" she deposited me at the curb of the Kingston station. My train was delayed, but it was such a nice day that I went onto the platform and sat on a bench in the clean, fresh air.

Amtrak arrived about an hour and a half later. I boarded.

Now, I was alone and lulled into quietude by the train's engine. The scenery was not interesting enough to distract me from my thoughts revolving around the past three days.

I realized that it would be a long, long time before I visited Buffy again.

KENT JARRELL

You Can't Make Old Friends

A MEMOIR

The two old friends set out into a light chop on a gray day on Lake Sunapee, New Hampshire, swimming towards the lighthouse just off the distant point. Pete was feeling good again, a year out from a bone marrow transplant. Kent was in New England for a visit and always up for a swim. That's what they often did together.

At Goose Rocks Beach in Maine, they would time the tides and when the waters were fastest, go shooting out of the mouth of the Little River into the chill of the Atlantic Ocean. They had to be careful not to bang into the sharp rocks, but the thrill was always there and they would go again and again, laughing, and yelling in the rushing dark blue water.

On Cape Cod, after an afternoon round of golf, they would take Pete's pontoon boat out to where the Bass River poured into Nantucket Sound, and swim in circles in the still twilight.

They had known each other for more than 60 years. First met in nursery school, or was it kindergarten? Neither could remember. Despite long interruptions in their friendship, they watched each other's lives play out.

In high school, Pete introduced his girlfriend to Kent. Within a month or so, she moved on to Kent. Later, when Kent was laid off, on food stamps, looking for a job as a TV reporter, he moved into Pete's party house on the banks of Great Bay Estuary across from Portsmouth, New Hampshire. They created the game of "Bowling for Breakage" in the basement, using an empty wine bottle for the ball and beer bottles for the pins.

Kent went on to small cities in Maine and New York and finally landed in Washington, D.C., covering the White House, Congress, and matters of state in a city known for transactional relationships. A marriage, and then, a second one. Children, acquaintances, and a small amount of celebrity.

Pete created a company with two partners from the University of New Hampshire. He built a successful and rich life in a small town not far from the ocean. A girl from college became his wife, and two daughters were born and raised. Pete had a wide and eclectic circle of friends and was elected to the Board of Selectmen.

Pete was physical in all things: hockey with ice times at dawn, high-terrain skiing, and windsurfing on the open sea.

The last time I saw Pete, illness had worn him down into the stooped figure of a much older man. It was the wedding of his older daughter, and he had to be helped by his wife as he walked. After the reception toasts, I approached Pete as he stood at the head table, his head sagging, one shaking arm on a chair, the other on his cane.

"Pete, we are going to swim together again," I said. I wasn't sure Pete recognized me, until he said softly, "Kent. No, we won't. No swimming. Never again."

My arms went around Pete's shoulders. My eyes clouded with quick sharp tears. Suddenly, several other arms surrounded us. It was a huddle of friends, drawn by the sense of both immediate and impending grief.

On Lake Sunapee, Pete was a couple of lengths ahead. Kent was tiring. This was new water for him and the closer he got to the point, the more he could feel the pull and twists of a dark, deep current. He made his decision and yelled ahead, "Pete, I'm done, I gotta head back."

Pete nodded in acknowledgement and pushed on. Looking over his shoulder, Kent saw Pete's arms, rising and falling in an arc, silver spray blown up and whipped back by the wind.

PAULA SPURLIN PAIGE

The Babysitter

The baby screamed violently, his little face tomato-red, his platinum hair lighting up the dark hallway like dandelions gone to seed as he flung his head back and forth. He clutched at Kate, pulling away from his new French baby sitter, Françoise.

"You're going to the park now," Kate said, "and when you come back Nana will give you lunch."

Oliver went on thrashing and screaming.

Françoise said: *"Laissez-moi sortir.* He will stop when he doesn't see you anymore."

Kate nodded, prying off his plump little tentacle-like arms and legs, and Françoise got him out into the hallway. Kate closed the door and leaned against it, breathing hard, wiping her own tears as the screams went on, then were, finally, mercifully swallowed up by the elevator's creaky descent.

Kate was about to go out to the market; she had her granny cart ready, so that she looked like an old-fashioned Parisian housewife. She'd just give them time to get around the corner on their way to the garden. Then she hesitated. She went over to stand by the window, looking out at the courtyard, at the unusually cloudless blue sky, at the white cat named Claude sitting in a window in the apartment across the way, next to a pot of geraniums. What a nice place this was that her son and his wife had rented, but they didn't seem to spend much time here: he was buried most days at the Bibliothèque Nationale, working on his latest book; she worked in a neighborhood café on hers. And Oliver went off every morning with a series of teenaged babysitters, whom they'd declined to replace with Kate for the short time she was in Paris. Privately, Kate knew that her daughter-in-law found her too distracted or too slow to take care of a toddler amid the many dangers of Paris.

Claude blinked up at her in the June sun, and all of a sudden Kate thought: to hell with the market! She was only here for two weeks, and she wanted to see Oliver. She stowed the shopping cart in the kitchen, grabbed the paper, and walked down the circular staircase, out through the front courtyard with its ivy-covered buildings, where children kicking a soccer ball muttered "Bonjour!" as she went by. She knew where Françoise and Oliver had gone: the courtyard of the Hôpital St. Louis a block or so away.

The Rue du Faubourg du Temple was a vibrant, tacky street that seemed to be the cheap shoe capital of Paris. High platform sandals were piled on tables on the sidewalk; bright sundresses in patterns that made you seasick waved like banners in the breeze. Kate turned down a side street that led to the hospital, a mostly Muslim street full of small shops in front of which men stood smoking and staring at passersby. Once she saw a woman's face eclipsed by a black chador peering out from the darkness of a shop.

Up ahead loomed the hospital, with its gray slate roofs atop rose and beige patterned walls, like the Place des Vosges. She slipped around the car barrier and walked under the arch into the courtyard, a typically French green island of calm in the midst of the noise and hot cement of Paris. Ahead of her was an oval hillock planted with purple pansies and pink begonias, ringed by a gravel path and then grass, where children were actually permitted to run. Young mothers and nannies sat on stone benches, surveying their children or charges. A few hospital patients were sitting out, too, in the morning sun, one an evident burn victim in a wheelchair—the hospital specialized in dermatology. Kate spotted Oliver toddling around on the grass on the other side of the garden mound. Françoise sat talking nearby with another nanny.

Kate sat down on a bench from which she could see Oliver but not be seen by Françoise. At least, she hoped not. She put up her paper as a screen, pretending to read about Strauss-Kahn and his humiliating treatment by the New York City police. Peering around the edge of the paper, she saw Oliver trip and tumble. Françoise called out "Olivier!" She came to scoop him up and they passed out of Kate's sight behind the flowered mound.

A few minutes later, Oliver set forth again. This time, he went farther afield, headed for the figure in the wheelchair, swathed in bandages, who had wheeled himself closer to Kate. The man—the gray hair looked like a man's—was smoking, inserting his cigarette among the bandages that crisscrossed his face. Only in France, Kate thought! Oliver watched in fascination, standing a few feet away, staring at this strange figure, at the cigarette going into the dark hole, at the blue smoke rising in the sunlight. It was quite possible that this privileged child of Northern California had never seen anyone smoke before. And then the man seemed to speak to Oliver, holding his cigarette to one side. Kate heard something that ended in *"mon petit prince."* Despite the bandages, Oliver smiled.

Kate stood and walked a bit closer. She saw that Françoise was absorbed in texting, and that the man was perfectly presentable. In fact, he seemed to have a rather aristocratic way of speaking, and he wore a green silk ascot around his neck. He acknowledged her from a distance: "Madame." It was a lovely moment.

All of a sudden, the man seemed to nod off, and dropped his cigarette on the grass beside him. Oliver stood transfixed for a moment or two, then began to run toward the spot of flame glowing in the grass. Kate did, too.

"Oliver!" she yelled, before Françoise had any idea what was going on (she was still texting, and jumped up in surprise when she saw Kate running around, and indeed through, part of the flowerbed). The baby stopped and turned; then his face lit up in a grin and he toddled to meet Kate.

"Na-na!" he cried. It was the first real word she'd ever heard him say. She caught him up in her arms.

Then the force of French society came down on her: Françoise came over to claim her charge, looking daggers at Kate because she probably thought she was a spy planted by her son, but also a bit shamefaced, as well she should. A dark-skinned gardener dressed in green appeared out of nowhere, berating Kate for walking on the *parterre*, gesturing at the crushed flowers. In vain did she plead that her *petit fils* was in danger of being burned by a cigarette butt; the gardener looked at her skeptically and handed her a fine for 25 euros, payable to the City of Paris.

But the man in the wheelchair moved in, speaking with the authority of the privileged. *"Je suis désolé, Madame.* This is all my fault. Permit me." He reached into the pocket of his pants—very nice gray flannel pants-- and pulled 25 euros out of a brown Hermès billfold, which he handed to her. Then he bowed and wheeled himself away.

Françoise was still standing there, looking at Kate warily, hot and flustered in her tight jeans and long-sleeved shirt.

"I wasn't spying. I just wanted to watch him," Kate said. "I don't get to see him very often. That's why I followed you."

Françoise's hazel eyes widened in surprise. "Really? You mean you're not going to tell your son?"

Kate laughed. "No." What a dark view of human nature the French had!

The girl smiled and handed her the baby. Kate stood holding him, inhaling his infant smell of new skin, powder, and poop. Then she kissed him, handed him back to Françoise and went off to make lunch.

Originally published in *A Diverse Arts Project.* © 2016

JUDITH BANNON SNOW

That Dragon!

Despite having three advanced degrees, I am becoming increasingly challenged by the *salami* (tsunami) of software that only sometimes works. My typing is agonizingly slow. Writing and editing take *and ordinarily* (inordinately) longer than they should. Chalk it up to *were* (poor) fine motor control.

Dragon NaturallySpeaking claims to obviate the need for any typing at all—you just talk. The speech recognition software program purportedly lets the user dictate text instead of typing it. Once *Dragon* learns the voice of the user, it then professes to seamlessly and flawlessly put the spoken words on the printed page. What could be better for those of us who are challenged with poor fine motor control skills? It is a clear-cut case where technology is your new best friend!

If the reader is confused by the preceding *texts* (text), let me *know* (note) that the things I dictated are in parentheses; the things *Dragon* chose to write instead are in italics.

My husband, tired of hearing incessant complaining as I write, losing me to the computer for hours on end, and inconvenienced by my frequent late arrivals at the dinner table, gave me *Dragon* as a gift.

Speaking instead of typing? Perfect. Unfortunately, *Dragon* and I aren't always on the same page. Often he (just to be clear, *Dragon* is definitely a "he") doesn't seem to understand, or maybe just doesn't care. Even worse, *Dragon* puts words in my mouth.

I *didn't* (did) the tutorial for 20 minutes before beginning to write. Corrections with *Dragon* were arduous. For example, "too"—repeated attempts to correct it produced *"to"* or *"two,"* but never "too."

Thinking (thanking) my husband for the gift, I remarked that it would be easier to correct by hand. He disagreed, saying that with practice, it is simpler with Dragon.

More frustrations: *Dragon's* microphone keeps turning off by itself. So I say *pick up* (wake up). Sometimes it does, sometimes it types "wake up" and sometimes it just ignores me.

Dragon completely ignores extra spaces. It capitalizes words at random. Why hasn't dedicated dictation software like *red* (the) *Dragon* mastered these simple skills?

It's egotistical enough to always capitalize its own name, *Dragon.*

I've just wasted five minutes trying to undo a change I made by *diluting* (deleting) some of the text. *Dragon will* (won't) let me undo it.

I didn't actually finish the tutorial. Not my fault, because during the *boreal* (tutorial) *Dragon* interrupted me via the Internet to update my new, just-out-of-the-box *Dragon* software.

"Dragon, can you hear me? Yes? Where were you 30 seconds ago? Do you have selective hearing loss?"

While searching for a flourish to separate the text, I realized this document wasn't saved. Couldn't find it because the *Moorish* (flourish), not Moorish, but *florists* (flourish), no, not florists, but *Irish* (flourish)—no, not Irish, but *British* (flourish)…

I give up, *Dragon.* Is flourish so difficult to understand? Especially when you got it right the first time? I couldn't find this document because flourish.docx had taken its place.

We need to discuss our relationship. Just when I'm thinking *were* (we're) good, you let me down. Your quirky interpretations of my words are harming our promising new friendship. Because you waste so much of my time, you are damaging my relationship with my husband. If that is your intent, it's a dastardly thing to do. I think you *are* (ought) to rethink your attitude—just *stand* (sayin').

Heedless *Dragon*—BTW, what is "How to Train Your Dragon?"

MICHAEL J. GORDON

On the Loss of a Child

A MEMOIR

Sitting on my desk is the last photo ever taken of our youngest son, Joel. A few days after it was taken, he was dead. He was twenty-six years old.

It is early winter. He is standing in the doorway of a Manhattan office building, wearing a long, black wool overcoat, collar turned up against the cold. The camera catches him smiling shyly. A cigarette is half-hidden in his hand, as if to conceal it from his parents who objected to him smoking.

Joel had moved to New York City three years before, intent on a career in banquet and event management. A summer job at a banquet facility after his freshman year of college convinced him that it was the line of work for him. To his parents' dismay, he chose to leave school and try his hand at it full time.

Once summer was over, however, jobs in that field were scarce in Connecticut. So off he went to the presumably better opportunities in New York, only to find that the banquet and event business was in the doldrums there as well. To make ends meet, he found a job in a store selling up-market American crafts. It was a good fit, as he was a talented sculptor himself, and could talk knowledgeably about the hand-made objects with customers.

Finally, he landed a job as Assistant Banquet Manager at Guastavino's, a high-end restaurant and catering establishment in Manhattan. It was located in an official New York Landmark, a beautifully tiled arcade with Catalan vaults under the Fifty-Ninth Street Bridge approach. The restaurant occupied the first floor. The private function rooms were on the second.

Joel enjoyed working there, and they liked him. He was soon planning Broadway opening night parties, and his company's participation in the annual Taste of New York.

Through his work, he met several celebrities. One he was particularly fond of was Lisa Kudrow, then a big star in her role as the ditzy blonde Phoebe on the television show Friends. He said she was down to earth with no airs. For an instant, his mother, Joan, and I got our hopes up—finally, a nice Jewish girl in his life—but then he said no, she was thirteen years his senior and already happily married.

On his way to work the morning of January 13, 2003, Joel boarded the subway. Somewhere under the streets of Brooklyn, he collapsed and died.

Joel shared an apartment in New York with our middle son, Seth. Joan and I had spent the day before there with them, something we got to do all too little. It was a Sunday, they both had the day off, and we actually found on-street parking near our rendezvous point in Greenwich Village.

The scene plays over and over in my mind: two tall figures walking toward us from the subway, Seth in a leather jacket, Joel in his long overcoat, each carrying a paper cup of coffee, steam curling up into the chill winter air.

It was bright and fair, and we spent the afternoon walking and talking, keeping to the sunny sides of the streets, ducking in and out of shops whenever the steady, biting wind became uncomfortable. The Strand Bookstore provided a good hour's shelter.

Both boys had become serious foodies after moving to New York, and we ate at a small Italian restaurant they had wanted to try. The food was good, we talked and walked some more, and then it was time to leave for home.

It had been a pleasant day—it was always good to see them.

The call came from Seth at nine-thirty the next morning: "The Woodhull Medical Center in Brooklyn called. They said that Joel has been taken ill and you need to come right away, but they said not to speed or drive recklessly."

The fear was immediate. *Taken ill.* With what? We had just seen him yesterday and he was fine. *Do not speed or drive recklessly.* That seemed to imply he wasn't in immediate danger. But then why the warning? *You need to come right away.* If he had been struck by a car, or been mugged, wouldn't they have told us? And not called it "taken ill?" *Joel has been taken ill.* Despite trying to keep from thinking the worst, we had two-and-a-half hours, one-hundred-thirty-five miles, of wondering and dread before us.

We were forty minutes from home when the cell phone rang. It was Seth again.

"Mom! Dad! He's dead! Joel's dead!"

I should have fallen apart right there on the Connecticut Turnpike, crashed into a guard rail or careened off the road, but I remember being immediately and completely overtaken by a need to be protective and reassuring. I told Seth to stay calm, that we were on the way. As I spoke, I had the curious and completely irrational thought that when we got there, I could do something about it, that somehow I could undo time and make Joel not dead. The thought lasted only for as long as it took to think it. Then reality sank in.

Joan and I went completely numb. I don't know how I was able to steer the car. It was past time for dread. The worst had already happened. No more fears, just an overwhelming, all-encompassing sadness, a sense of unutterable loss, and a complete hollowing out of our souls.

After taking a wrong exit in Brooklyn, we finally arrived at the hospital. Seth was at the door, waiting for us. The three of us hugged, cried, and went inside.

We pieced the story together. Joel was on his way to work, riding the subway from Brooklyn to Manhattan, when he collapsed onto the floor of the train. An ambulance was called at the next stop, but it was too late, too late for the EMTs to revive him. He was gone well before he arrived at the hospital.

The Medical Center could provide no detailed information. Joel had collapsed, and then he died. Under New York City law, any unexplained death required an autopsy, and until then the hospital could give only the bare facts. Joel was, and now he wasn't.

Our first-born, Noah, flew home from the University of Missouri, where he was working on his PhD. The funeral was two days later, when the Medical Examiner released the body. The autopsy itself would take six additional months. During that time, I spoke to the pathologist on the case nearly every week. In the end, she could find nothing. No heart trouble. No stroke. No drugs. No virus. No bacteria. Nothing that would have caused death.

Except, there was no Joel.

The funeral filled the synagogue. Joel's friends, our friends and relatives. Local people, of course, but others driving or flying in from around the country. Condolence calls from Jerusalem and Cairo. Our rabbi conducted the service. I was unable to speak, as was Joan, but Noah and Seth did, and some of Joel's friends offered remembrances. A rabbi we knew from a nearby town read a poem about how the soul is like a ship sailing off to sea—while it seems smaller and smaller the farther it gets from our shore, the larger it becomes to someone waiting on the far side. As much as was possible under the circumstances, it was a comforting thought. I asked him about it afterward. He said he had lost the poem years before, and had just found it again that very morning.

In a remarkable instance of how small a city of seven million can be, about a month afterward, a friend of Joel's in New York was telling the story to a friend of hers. That friend had just heard an almost identical account from a man who had been on the train and attempted to help. Phone numbers were exchanged, and I was able to speak with him. He was a police officer, still in civvies on his way to work himself that morning. He described Joel as having a lost and puzzled look on his face as he lay on the floor. The officer had tried to help, but obviously to no avail.

For the seven days after the funeral, we sat shiva, the traditional week-long, initial Jewish mourning period. The house was filled with visitors making condolence calls, coming to offer moral support. Many brought food, some complete meals.

After that, Noah and Seth returned to their lives in Missouri and New York, respectively. Some time later, we stopped rereading the condolence cards and funeral home sign-in books. We had continued to look at them not to remind ourselves of who was at the funeral, or who may have shared some of our grief, but as a way of hanging on to the last time we spent with Joel, even though he was already gone. On a suggestion from a cousin (coincidentally, also named Joel), we got a separate, temporary phone line, attached a recording device, and invited any friends and relatives so inclined to leave audio memories. A few did. Following tradition, for a year I attended synagogue services not only on the Sabbath, but also for the short, daily minyans to recite the mourner's kaddish prayer. Whether it was the praying, or slowly gaining strength from the routine of acknowledging the loss every day, it seemed to help.

Our lives would never, could never, be the same again. Still, slowly over the weeks and months the rhythm, the format of our days began to more closely resemble what they had been before. We tried to hold in our emotions (not the best idea, the books tell you), to attempt to be strong for each other. Neither one wanted to keep reminding the other of our loss—as if it were possible to forget.

Joan resumed her work writing restaurant reviews. She'd had several weekly columns in reserve when Joel died. When they ran out, the paper reprinted old pieces until she was ready to return—but frankly food, like the rest of our lives, had lost all flavor.

My business partner took care of my clients until, getting antsy, I went back to work, trying to go through the motions. I did a lot of staring out of the window.

Returning to weekly Rotary Club meetings, and working on its charitable projects, was beneficial. It wasn't the way I'd ever want the adage to be proven, but concentrating on helping others, which is what Rotary does, helped me as well.

That summer, one of Joel's musical compositions he had recorded was used for a recital number at the Jacob's Pillow Dance Center in Massachusetts. A good friend of his had suggested the music to whoever was setting up the program. Joan and I went, of course, accompanied by nearly a dozen of our friends who came to offer moral support. The two of us sobbed all the way through.

It has been a long time now, but there will never be enough of it. Time cannot heal. The best it can do is let you become more accustomed to the loss, and to learn to live with it. We may still choke up whenever we have to refer to our "late" son, but the world, our lives, and the lives of our other sons (and now a grandson) move ever on. Yet years later, every single day we see or hear at least one thing that makes us think of Joel—something he made, a piece of music he might have enjoyed—things impossible to see or hear without a twinge of wonder of what might have been.

Excerpted from book-length memoir
Stringy Brisket: A Restaurant Critic's Spouse, soon to be published.

JUDITH M. COOKE

One Button Off

As is true of many things, the outside of the Wilburt State Psychiatric Hospital was dramatically different from the inside. From the parking lot to the front door of the residential building, the grounds were kept much like a private park, tranquil and lovely, with carefully planned gardens and landscaped sitting areas. Even the walkways were slabs of slate, laid in paths that meandered through the manicured lawns past a white gazebo and flowering shrubs. The Bronson Building was a dignified brownstone with tall, arched windows and rounded front steps. Immediately upon entering, though, all traces of Eden vanished, and there was no hiding that this was a grim place to live.

The lobby was tiled with grey-speckled, institutional flooring, the few straight-backed chairs along the wall were bolted down, and the three gray metal doors leading to the wards had wire criss-crossed through their small rectangular windows. The security guard glanced at my ID badge and nodded me through. Heavy gray doors had to be unlocked and relocked every leg of the journey to the wards, first at the bottom of the staircase, then at the top, and then onto the floors.

Bronson Two West was a geriatrics ward. Most of the patients spent their days in the sunroom, sitting and chain smoking while the television blared trash-talk-shows, where angry people screamed at one another. A few patients sat immobile, staring ahead at nothing, unable or unwilling to communicate. A scrawny woman with long gray hair tied into a single scraggly braid down her back crouched in the corner, rocking back and forth. Some others sat quietly, looking out the windows.

As I scanned the room for a good place to sit, a heavyset aide dressed all in white hoisted herself out of an orange vinyl chair. As she waddled across the room, I saw that her ID badge read "Tasha Jackson CNA."

"How long you gon' be here," she asked.

"About an hour," I said, trying to sound pleased to be on the ward.

"All righty then," she said, and left the room. State regulations said that a staff person had to be present wherever groups of patients gathered, so whenever I arrived, the aides seized the opportunity to take an extra break.

Trying to appear comfortable and approachable, I took a chair in one of the seating groups away from the television. An elderly man sat smiling and humming tunelessly to himself, his hair disheveled and his cardigan done up one button off. The person next to him might have been a woman – I really couldn't be sure. She – or he – had short salt and pepper hair and a barrel shaped torso, and wore khakis and an oversized red tee-shirt that read "Maryland is for Crabs."

Pasting what I hoped was a pleasant smile to my face, I asked the humming old man, "How are you today?"

The androgynous patient spoke instead. "Need a smoke. You got a smoke I can bum?"

"No. Sorry," I said. "I don't smoke."

"Then what good are you?" he – or maybe she – demanded in his – or was it her – gravelly voice.

With fifty-eight more minutes to go before I could leave, I tried again. "I'm one of the chaplains, and I'm here for anyone who wants to talk."

The patient looked at my ID badge. "Chaplain? You don't look like no chaplain."

"I hear that a lot," I said. "I'm Judith. And you are?"

"Bawb."

Did he say "Bob?" Or did she say "Barb?"

"So you come here to convert me? I don't need no converting. I'm a believer already. Got saved by a traveling preacher."

"Is that so?" I said.

"Yep," she – or he – told me. "I already know it all. Matthew Mark Luke John. The Alpha and the Omega. The Leggo my Eggo."

"The Leggo my Eggo?" I repeated.

Bawb looked exasperated. "You don't know about Jesus and the Leggo my Eggo?"

"I know Jesus," I said. "And Matthew, Mark, Luke, and John. And the Alpha and the Omega."

"What good are they without the Leggo my Eggo?" demanded Bawb. And shaking his – or her – head, Bawb got up and moved to a chair closer to the television.

Fifty-two minutes to go.

Taking a deep breath and turning to the elderly man who was still there, I smiled at him and said, "And how are you today?"

He smiled back, still humming to himself, but he didn't answer.

Even though I was supposed to talk to as many patients as I could, I stayed in my chair for ten minutes. The television was blaring so loudly I couldn't ignore it.

"And I'm not 'shamed of it neither," screeched a very pregnant blond girl from the screen. "I never loved you. I love him."

"That's sick," screamed back a skinny young man with a shaved head and jeans so big on him that three inches of his underwear showed at the waist. "Your brother? You *bleeeeeeep* your brother?"

"And this is his baby, not yours," she yelled at him, pointing to her belly.

"And it's time now to bring out the brother," said the host. "Come on out, Jack."

A balding man near the television stood up and pointed at

the girl on the screen. "I fucked her too. See that girl," he said gesturing wildly. "I fucked her. We all did. She's a tramp. She liked it."

"Allen!" said a burly male aide who had appeared from nowhere. "Settle down now."

"I fucked her. I swear it," Allen told him.

"Settle down," repeated the aide, his tan muscular arms crossed over his chest. "Or do you need to go to the quiet room?"

"No," said Allen, quickly returning to his seat. "No, I'm settled. No need. No need."

The aide stood in the doorway for a few more seconds, apparently to make sure the crowd was properly controlled. Looking to the corner where the skin-and-bones old lady still crouched, he said, "Caroline, you need to be in a chair."

The old lady didn't move.

"Caroline, come on now," he said to her. "In a chair."

Not quite loudly enough for me to hear, she croaked out a word or two to the aide.

"I know, but you still need a chair," he said, pulling her off the floor and into a vinyl seat, not as gently as someone would normally help up an old lady.

Then, the aide evidently decided that things were under control, and he left.

Thirty-five minutes left. Time to change seats. I moved to a table where two old men were playing cards and an elderly woman was watching.

"Mind if I sit with you awhile?" I asked.

"More the merrier," said one man, taking a card from the pile.

"I'm Judith, one of the chaplains," I told them.

"I'm Jim, and that's Marie and Sam," said the other man.

"How are you doing today?" I asked the group.

"Fine," they each answered and went back to their cards.

As I watched them draw and discard, I wished for the millionth time that I had taken a different assignment. I could be playing games with a youth group, or leading Bible Study with a roomful of church ladies. Even the job at the soup kitchen seemed better than this. Week after week was the same. I showed up on the wards for an hour every day, and no one cared if I was there or not. Since I was the youngest chaplain, I always dressed as professionally as I could, only to go back home frustrated and reeking of cigarette smoke. Even with nothing else to do, none of them wanted to have a conversation with me. These people had therapists and psychiatrists and endless drugs to help them. They had no use for a young, female, part-time chaplain.

Twelve minutes and I could go.

"See you later," I said, getting up and moving on. Looking over the prospects, I chose the chair next to Caroline, who was rocking back and forth.

"Good afternoon, Caroline," I said, hoping I sounded cheerier than I felt. "How are you today? "

In slow motion, she turned in her chair to face me. She wore a horrible flowered housedress that was at least two sizes too big for her and covered in stains. While her face had so many wrinkles that it was hard to know what she really looked like, her eyes were the brightest blue I'd ever seen. Clutching my wrist with both of her gnarled hands, she leaned in close and said very slowly, "I'm dead."

Not sure what the right response to this was, I stammered, "You…I…uh…well now, you don't look dead to me."

This was very clearly the wrong thing to say.

Caroline screamed, "I am! I am dead!" And she threw herself out of the chair and onto the floor, as though to prove to me that she was in fact deceased.

"Oh no," I babbled on. "I didn't mean…you can be dead, Caroline. You can be dead if you want. Let's get back in the chair now. Upsy-daisy."

But Caroline merely lay on the floor, curled on her side, her fingers twisted like claws.

Sitting on my heels next to her, I tried to talk in a soothing voice. "It's all right, Caroline. You're fine. Everything's fine. Time to get back in the chair."

Bawb trudged over and looked down at us both. Shaking his – or her – head in disgust, she – or he – screamed to the hallway, "Caroline's dead again."

A moment later, the male aide returned. "Every freakin' day," he grumbled. "Come on, Caroline. Back to your seat."

But Caroline just lay frozen, not even her eyes moving.

"I'm getting sick of this, Caroline," he said, a harsh edge in his voice. "You need to get back up. Now."

"I think this is my fault," I told him. "I said the wrong thing and now–"

"It's not you. She does this all day long," the aide told me, cracking the knuckles on his left hand. Then turning back to Caroline he said, "You know the rules. The state doesn't allow anyone to lie on the floor like this. You have to get up, or you have to go to the quiet room."

"Come on, Caroline," I tried. "You can do it. I'll help you up."

Slowly, slowly, her eyes moved to mine and she whispered, "I'm dead."

The aide shook his head. "That's it. Quiet room it is then."

Squatting down on his enormous haunches, he took her by the ankles. Then standing back up, he began hauling her out of the sunroom feet first. Her housedress bunched up around her hips, showing her pitifully skinny thighs and her graying underpants, her hair and arms trailing behind her on the floor. Caroline lay a motionless corpse as she was dragged down the hallway, while the aide grumbled comments like "sick and tired of this" and "no wonder you're locked up" and "damned crazies." At the end of the hall, another heavy gray door slammed, and they were gone.

Except for the couple screaming on the television, the sunroom had gone hauntingly silent. When a patient needed to go to the quiet room to calm down, either they walked on their own, or they were carried by several staff members. Never was anyone dragged. And Caroline was so old and frail, she looked like she could break a hip if someone just looked at her too hard. Nervous glances were exchanged between the patients who were looking up. Others were staring at the floor, as though pretending they weren't there. Only the catatonics seemed unaffected. No one made eye contact with me.

After a few minutes, the patients went back to their cards and conversations and television watching. With only two minutes left, I decided I could leave. But just as I started moving to the door, Bawb flopped into the seat that Caroline had occupied up until her most recent death.

"You know, Chaplain," he – or maybe she – said.

Sitting down again, I looked at Bawb. "Do I know what?"

"Sometimes the real crazies are the ones with the keys."

I nodded, not sure what to say.

Bawb looked at me and said, "Like you."

"Me?" I asked.

Bawb nodded with certainty. "You gotta be crazy to come here if you don't have to."

RAE STUDHOLME

Undercliff

A hierarchy of patients existed on the ward—"alkies," "druggies," "loonies." I was never really sure of their order of transcendence. Neither was my father, the patient, though it was all too clear to me, at least, into which group he belonged. Daddy, however, was never able to make that universal AA statement: "My name is Glenn, and I'm an alcoholic." So he and I pretended it was perfectly normal for a 16-year-old girl to spend long, sunless afternoons playing cribbage with quivering, newly-sober drunks in a state mental hospital. Other girls hung out at the mall. I hung out at Undercliff.

My father's hands—hands that had pounded out innumerable fenders, written flawless Palmer script notes to my teachers, held my hand—shook relentlessly and recklessly. His hands, like his drinking, were out of control. He'd say, "Fifteen for two," easily enough. But steadying his fingers to peg the points on the cribbage board was a major challenge.

"They're sure making these holes small these days," he'd joke, half-heartedly.

"You must be drinking too much coffee, Daddy," I'd lie.

Daddy would light another Kool, unfiltered, and place his ancient, dented Zippo on the table.

"Your deal," he exhaled. "That damn fool Donny drank a bottle of Aqua Velva last night. Damn fool. Had to get his stomach pumped. It'll be a cold night in hell before they catch me downing a bottle of after-shave."

Vodka was your poison, Daddy. You would stash half-drunk

bottles of Smirnoff in the snow banks lining our driveway. And in the spring thaw, the ground under the forsythias would be littered with glass pints competing with the crocuses.

Men outnumbered women at Undercliff twenty-to-one. As far as I could tell, the sexes never mingled. Most of the women at the hospital were there for mental health issues and the "loonies" weren't interested in sex, my father informed me.

"They don't even talk to anyone but themselves. It's a cacophony of never-ending soliloquies even after they get their little white paper cups of medications. You won't ever catch me talking my own god damned self, Rae Marie!"

The "druggies" on the ward were, on the whole, young men desperate to avoid the Vietnam War, and willing to risk ODing on Thorozine, LSD, or heroin in order to escape the draft. Many of the recovering alcoholics, my father included, were Word War II veterans who had little tolerance for "those long-haired weirdos." I never told Daddy I knew more than one of those boys on his ward.

Wives visited mainly on Sundays. My father and mother had divorced the year before Daddy entered "treatment" for the first time, but my mother still visited him every Sunday.

"I was married to him for eighteen years. How can I desert him now when he's finally drying out?" she'd tell her bewildered, inquisitive friends.

My mother always dressed up for her visit—hose, high-heels, and a dress or skirt. She was a stark contrast to the female patients who shuffled along in hospital slippers and food-stained robes. My mother always attracted the attention of men, and the men of Undercliff were no exception. Bizarrely, a few years later, when I left home, my mother married one of my father's fellow patients.

Treatment at Undercliff consisted of daily AA meetings, during which my father refused to acknowledge his addiction, weekly group therapy or "bull-sessions" as my father called them, heavy doses of Antabuse, and sporadic consultations with the lone, over-worked resident psychiatrist. The underlying strategy of Undercliff's recovery program was detoxification and incarceration. Since my father never admitted he had a drinking problem, there was little impact on his ability to stay on the wagon the many times he was released. But he was well-liked at the hospital by both the inmates and the staff. Maybe that's part of why he kept going back to Undercliff. Daddy spent considerable time at that institution during the late 1960's. In the closing years of that decade my father still had his sense of humor, his cache of stories to tell, and at least a small amount of self-respect. But later, when the calendars turned to the '70s, those traits left him, too.

Daddy always earned his way into the Day Release Work Program quickly. He had a skill and a large number of former employers who would vouch for him and give him a job as an auto body man. But whenever he was discharged completely, those same work buddies would invariably become drinking buddies again. Without the security and control of the ward, the lure of the bottle was too much for him. The concept of a half-way house had not yet come to our working-class area of Connecticut. Sponsors were a part of AA, which my father despised. "Higher power, my ass," he'd say. Daddy was not a religious man.

The first time my father was released from Undercliff, my mother insisted he stay at our house, albeit platonically. It wasn't long before my father was eating SenSen mints to cover the smell of booze on his breath. One night he came home with a bloody nose and no recollection of how it had happened. Rather than let him sleep it off on the couch, our usual response to his benders, my mother and I drove him, drunk and bleeding, back to the ward. It was a trip with which we became intimately familiar.

At some point, my mother had enough. She no longer held even a sliver of hope that my father would ever be able to stop drinking. So, on his next discharge, my mother bought him new clothes and a one-way ticket to California, where my grandmother, his mother, lived. My mother, my father and I drove to the airport quietly. We watched him board the plane, and I never saw my father again.

I, too, left Connecticut. Not for California, but for Colorado. Even now, when I see used-men like my dad living on the streets, under the bridges of Boulder Creek, trudging up Broadway to the homeless shelter, hustling quarters for another pint of Smirnoff, I swallow my heart. Whose father, brother, husband, son are they? Am I guilty because I'm relieved my daddy is dead? And who's dealing the cards at Undercliff now?

ISABELLE DOUGLAS SEGGERMAN

Flipping Their Lids

The kitchen in our historic house is small, but extraordinarily well planned and laid out. It was redesigned in the 1960s by someone I have assumed was trained as a marine architect. Everything is situated within reach; the stove is exactly 29" behind the dishwasher, placed in the center island. The fridge is to the right of the 66" long island, about an arm's length away. A cubby with sliding door holding the spices is about a foot left of the stove. There are many cabinets, each designed to hold specific items such as trays, paper grocery bags—or whatever— within their perfectly planned spaces. My kitchen is compact, practical and easy to cook in—as long as there are not too many cooks in it at the same time.

The FedEx man delivered a very large box last Friday. I assumed it was something my daughter had ordered. The next day another delivery man brought another big cardboard carton; again, I assumed it was something that my adult child had ordered for herself.

I was right on the first count. When she and I spoke on Sunday night she informed me that she had ordered them. However, they were not for herself, but rather for me. She told me to open them, which I tackled the next morning, as the cartons were big and would leave behind a lot of cardboard to discard afterwards.

The first contained a very modern looking, brushed metal, rectangular garbage can with a snugly fitting black top that contained several push buttons. The second box contained its twin. Now, for the first time ever, I possessed a matching set: a can for the wet garbage as well as a can for the recyclables. However, along with these new cans came a pack of size D batteries. Following the packages' directions, I carefully placed two batteries in the top of each lid. Then it all began…

As I walked by the first can, which I had placed in front of the island opposite to the eating area, the lid opened of its own accord. When my cocker spaniel explored the second can, which was in between the back kitchen wall and the right side of the island, it also opened. This happened throughout the morning whenever there was motion in front of the cans—or so I thought. I began to experiment with these unrequested modern wonders.

When I moved my hand over each, one a green light would flash and the lid would miraculously open. A red light would then flash and the lid would decide to close itself. My husband wasn't as enchanted with the magic motions as my spaniel and I were.

In order not to wear down the batteries, or my husband's tolerance of these magically opening receptacles, I moved the cans and turned them both towards the rear wall. It seemed to make sense, although now there was no space left to move in front of them. However, the automatic lid flipping continued. Each time I reached over one to get to the microwave on the rear counter, one or the other would open. When I waved my hand over them, one or the other—or both—would open and then close at the time of its own choosing. When the electric coffee grinder cord dangled from the counter, the nearest one would open.

Although they were far more attractive than the Wedgewood blue plastic one and the broken metal one they had replaced, and a tiny bit taller, they were also narrower. The first time I opened one to remove its contents to take to the dump, I had to lift my arms up to my shoulders to get enough leverage to pull the plastic bag liners out. With man vs. machine determination, the bags were removed in about ten minutes (far too much time for a "modern convenience"). Cans emptied, off to the dump I went with the contents.

When I returned, the lids were exactly where they had been left, on top of the back kitchen counters. Then it began all over again. Both lids began to open and close regardless of the fact that they weren't even on the cans. Up and down, up and down, the lights flickering green and red, green and red.

It's now been a week of ups and downs, but I have figured out a formula to outsmart the cans. The first trick is to stand behind each one, and lift its lid by hand from the rear. Voila! No movement. I could remove the batteries as well, but feel my daughter's feelings might get hurt. Better to let them run out on their own and "forget" to replace them. I can also stand to the side of each one, avoiding any physical motion over the tops and do a sneak attack hand lift from their sides.

On the other hand, the spaniel and I have grown accustomed to the lids, and my husband simply ignores them. The lids, on the other hand, continue to open and close to their own beat. The red light seems to flash for no reason, while the green one flashes off and on at will.

MICHAEL J. GORDON

No Hits, No Runs...No Eros?

The very first time Norman fell in love—deeply, truly, hopelessly in love—he was eleven years old. The object of his all-consuming affection was a girl named Noreen who sat two rows away and three seats ahead in school. Every afternoon Norman waited for the sun to come around to the sixth grade side of the building, waited for it to shine through the window and outline Noreen's face with a soft, golden glow. He knew they must have been made for each other. After all, fate had decreed that they be given similar first names.

His infatuation lasted for about three months, until one day he saw her picking her nose right out in the open on the sidewalk in front of the school. By then, most of the boys had learned not to perform that particular act in public—at least not in view of any girls. Of course, girls got boogers, too, but they were supposed to remove them with a handkerchief, or at least in private, not stick their fingers up their noses out where everybody could see. His idol, the girl he had admired, the vision daily bathed in the glow of sixth grade afternoon sunlight, turned out to have been made of clay.

It was two years before Norman fell in love again. He liked certain girls from time to time, but even at that age he knew that there was a difference between like and love. In the eighth grade, however, he was suddenly moonstruck over a new girl, Caroline, who was very pretty, had a bubbly personality, and was the acknowledged class athlete besides.

To his delight, she reciprocated his interest, and they were boyfriend and girlfriend all the way through June. Then she went away for the summer, while he mowed lawns to earn spending money. By fall, when they started at their big regional high school, it was all over. They shared none of the same classes, and hardly saw each other. Caroline started dating a boy who could drive.

During those first few weeks of high school, Norman was awestruck over how many pretty girls there were—in class, the halls, the gym, in the cafeteria. He dated often over the next four years, a couple of times on a more-or-less steady basis. None of those relationships lasted very long, however.

He went to college at Arizona State University, not far from his home, and studied evolutionary biology. An outgoing young man, he found no lack of friendly companionship among the co-eds. A fan of Broadway musicals, he joined the school's main theater troupe. Besides the fun and excitement, it was a good way to meet girls.

Unlike most of his male cohort, however, he did not engage in the courtship dance solely for the physical thrills it might provide.

For Norman was still looking for love. It had been a long time since he felt as he had about Noreen, or for the entire eighth grade about Caroline, a time when two fourteen-year-olds could see no other partners in their futures, and talked about what life would be like when they were married. Now, five years later, it seemed forever since he had been suffused with such an indefinable, all-encompassing warmth, and he missed it.

While Norman was growing up in the hot southwest, far to the east a girl named Felicity was doing the same in the hills of New England. When she was a small child, she was so strikingly beautiful that total strangers would stop her parents to ask when they were taking her to Hollywood. By the time she finished grade school, she was a tall, quiet, dark-haired beauty, who loved to hike in the woods, and when the snow fell, to ski back-country trails.

In high school, she was a serious student, eager to learn. Her favorite subject was English, especially literature. She devoured The Forsythe Saga as a freshman, and became a fan of Elizabeth Barrett Browning. After receiving a driver's license at sixteen, her first trip alone was a ninety-minute excursion to Amherst to visit Emily Dickinson's home.

Although popular with the boys—they couldn't help but be struck by her looks—she didn't have any particular beaux. As much as she wished for someone to sweep her off her feet, none did. She read Jane Austen and the Brontë sisters, and began to write her own poetry.

Her writing was good enough to win her scholarship offers from several universities. She chose Mount Holyoke College because, however briefly, it was the school Emily Dickinson had attended, back when it was called the Mount Holyoke Female Seminary.

When she and the other freshman girls arrived on campus, they were met by a swarm of boys from Amherst College and the University of Massachusetts, offering to help carry the new students' possessions up to their rooms. Every weekend there seemed to be one party after another, and she was asked out frequently. Although most of the boys seemed nice, she quickly learned to spot the ones interested in just one thing—most were not very smooth in trying to attain it.

Felicity studied English, especially the major poets. Their ideas, their rhythms, their uses of language thrilled her. It was a good thing, she supposed, because none of the boys she'd met in nearly four years of college had done the same. She had liked some, even gave fleeting thought to what it would be like to be married to one or two. But none of them measured up to those she had met in literature, ones who were genuine lovers—even if they had been dead for over a hundred years. She couldn't help getting a twinge of sadness that she, at twenty-one, had never felt that way about someone herself.

Emily Dickinson, Felicity's inspiration for attending Mt.

Holyoke, had wound up never married, hardly ever leaving the house, and dying a recluse. Felicity had no intention of doing the same. She'd find someone, someday. Of that, she was sure.

The time went swiftly, and suddenly commencement was just a month away. Felicity's college friends would be going their separate ways. She'd miss the camaraderie, the constant gossip about boys, the buzzing about which girls were doing what with whom. Several classmates were engaged, and planning to get married over the summer; she'd been asked to be a bridesmaid for three. Those girls would go wherever their future husbands' jobs took them.

At Mount Holyoke, Felicity had acted in several productions, and like so many bitten by the theater bug, headed for New York after graduation to try to break into show business. At this (again, like most) she was completely unsuccessful. Six months later, rapidly running out of money, she interviewed for a "real" job, one for which four years of studying the great poets had made her well-prepared—writing jingles for an ad agency. She could still go to theater auditions at night, she reasoned.

That same month, Norman completed a Master's degree in Ecology, and accepted a job with the Schuylkill River Conservancy, an environmental protection agency based in Philadelphia. He planned to work for a couple of years, and then go back to school for a PhD.

Norman enjoyed living in the City of Brotherly Love. It wasn't as spread out as Phoenix, and most days he took pleasure in being able to walk down historic streets to his job—as well as to pretty much everything else going on in town. The social scene for twenty-somethings was lively, and he never missed one of the rare occasions when a theater would host an out of town tryout for an aspiring Broadway show.

All the while, he kept a steady eye out for Miss Right.

At work, he particularly enjoyed the days he was able to get out in the field, driving or boating along the Schuylkill. His main duties, however, involved trying to persuade various government agencies to support the plans his group devised to improve the environment along the waterway—or to prevent government bureaucrats from taking actions that would make it worse. Occasionally, this required him to travel out of town.

It was on such a mission that early one morning he boarded the train at 30th Street Station in Philadelphia, bound for the regional office of the Army Corps of Engineers in New York. (Despite the seeming illogic, the Army, not the Navy, has jurisdiction over United States navigable waterways.)

Arriving in New York's Pennsylvania Station, Norman followed the signs toward the subway that would take him to within walking distance of his destination. Ambling through the concourse, he paused to look at the plain spaces and dull ceilings of the renovated station. He had seen enough photos of the original station's interior—dramatic and handsome, a true railroad cathedral of soaring metal arches and expanses of glass—to be disgusted by what had replaced it in the name of modernization. On his occasional sojourns through it, he walked slowly, imagining what it must have been like in the old days, feeling a pang of sorrow for the former grandeur he had never seen in person, and for what had befallen the place.

He had an hour to go before his meeting, and as he dawdled along a beautiful young woman with dark hair entered the concourse from the exact subway portal toward which he was headed. Surrounded by the rush hour crowd hurrying toward the exits, she turned away and into a small shop, emerging no more than a minute later carrying a bag with a bagel inside. Had she not stopped, she might have seen the tall young man nearby, standing with his neck oddly craned back, looking disapprovingly at the ceiling.

But she did stop, and while she was paying for her bagel he was disappearing down the subway stairs.

STRIKE ONE.

The astute reader will no doubt realize that had their timing been just slightly different, the subjects of this story would have found themselves standing within full view of each other. Furthermore, you may take on faith the author's testimony that if the two had indeed set eyes upon one another, they would have been awestruck and fallen madly in love on the spot.

But they didn't.

Following his meeting with the guardians of the waterways, Norman took the subway north, up to midtown Manhattan. He was on his way to meet a friend for lunch on Madison Avenue, after which he planned to walk back to the station to catch a train home.

Norman's friend was his old college roommate, who shortly after his arrival three years ago had been tapped as an up-and-coming hotshot at a venerable Manhattan financial firm. In keeping with this status, he had reserved a table near the window at an au currant, ultra-trendy restaurant.

"Don't get scared by the prices," he told Norman as they sat down, "I have a company credit card."

The food was precious, both in cost and execution. (Taste was another story, but not wanting to spoil his friend's hospitality and demonstration of his success, Norman did not mention that he would have been happier with a good Philadelphia cheese steak.) The two young men laughed while talking over old times, how work was going, and the status of their current love lives. Smiling, Norman's friend described his as "active." He was having the time of his life as a well-off bachelor in the Big Apple.

"There's been only one little glitch," his friend said. "Frankly, I never thought I'd be in this situation vis-a-vis women, because I never dreamed I'd be in such good financial shape. Anyway, every now and then I get the distinct feeling that some babe is looking right through me, and x-raying my wallet. I suppose that goes with being single and owning a Porsche in Manhattan."

Smiling, he added, "Maybe it's tit for tat, if you'll pardon the expression. We stare at their boobs, they stare at our checkbooks.

Or something like that. Doesn't make any difference, though. I am far from when I might be looking for love or marriage. How about you?"

Norman, who in contrast had been looking for love since the sixth grade, replied that the social life in Philadelphia was just okay.

"I haven't met nearly as many girls as you have. With my job, certainly none are going to be attracted by my modest salary, much less be impressed by a six-year-old Subaru."

His friend chuckled, and said, "Norman, why don't you come up here for a weekend? We'll have a party. I'll invite some unbelievable women."

"Could I afford to meet them?" Norman joked.

His friend paid the lunch bill, which Norman estimated would cover a month's rent on his apartment in Philadelphia. Then the two men left, promising to get together again soon.

His friend headed toward his office and investments, while Norman turned in the direction of the train station, and his—in comparison—quiet social life.

Not ten seconds later, a beautiful brunette walking a half-block behind Norman passed the restaurant. Recognizing it as one currently being touted in the press as catering to the hip and the wannabes, she briefly glanced through the window as she passed by.

Fleetingly speculating on whether the food was any good, she imagined that the only way she would find out would be on the arm of some show-off with more money than brains. Looking at the back of the man walking ahead of her, she wondered whether he was one of those.

The young woman, of course, was Felicity, the one whose bagel purchase that morning had thwarted meeting Norman in the Pennsylvania Station concourse. Now, returning from a lunchtime walk, she continued a little way behind him. Being tall, with a long stride, she was used to overtaking other pedestrians on the sidewalk, but although the man in front momentarily paused a couple of times to look in shop windows, she never got a look at his face before having to turn into the building wherein she would write her afternoon quota of jingles.

Norman, of course, kept walking on toward the station.

STRIKE TWO.

What's up with these two nice people? The author keeps trying to put them where they will meet, but they insist on going off on their own. It's very frustrating for a writer.

Returning home after work, Felicity extracted the mail from her box in the downstairs hall before climbing the two flights to her one-room apartment. Inside, she took a started bottle of burgundy from the fridge, and poured herself a healthy glass. Then she dropped down on the couch, kicked off her shoes, and casually looked through what the postman had brought.

Most of it was the usual junk, but among the magazines and flyers was a letter from a publisher in Philadelphia. She recognized the name as one for which her firm had done some advertising. But why were they writing her at home, instead of the office? Opening the envelope, she found a letter from the publisher's vice-president, whom she had met at a recent booksellers' conference. He was writing to inquire whether she'd be interested in a job in Philadelphia, one with a nice increase in pay.

Surprised and flattered to receive an offer out of the blue, Felicity spent the evening thinking it over. The next morning, she called the man to discuss exactly what the job entailed, and he invited her to visit the publishing house and see for herself.

They agreed on a day later that week.

On his way back to Philadelphia on the train, Norman reflected on how much he liked New York, its bustle, and hordes of well-dressed, attractive young women. He liked his current job, but it never hurt to look, and he had developed a habit of scanning the "positions available" in every issue of the professional publications. He knew the job prospects in New York were good, and although the cost of living was higher, the salaries were as well.

"Why not?" he thought to himself. He even had a place to bunk while looking. His friend would let him stay with him in the bachelor condominium near Lincoln Center until he got settled on his own.

So it was that Norman interviewed for several jobs, was offered three, and accepted the best one.

Maybe in New York he'd meet the girl of his dreams.

In the meantime, Felicity visited Philadelphia, was interviewed by the publisher's CEO, and was offered and accepted a position as a copy editor. Her jingle-writing days were over.

It was a good job, in a new town for her. Maybe she'd meet a man there, perhaps a budding Shelley or Keats, even a knight on a white horse who would sweep her off her feet—someone with whom she would fall in love. In that respect, New York had been a washout.

And so Norman and Felicity switched cities of residence. Coincidentally, one day their moving trucks passed within sight of each other, going in opposite directions on the New Jersey Turnpike.

STRIKE THREE?

Perhaps not. Two years hence Norman and Felicity will both accept jobs in Boston, where their offices will be in adjacent buildings on Tremont Street.

The author has done all he can, and wishes them luck. As he has said, they will make a perfect couple—if they ever meet, which he fervently hopes they will.

JENNIFER J. FRANCHERE

Fred and the Car Wash

Fred left his building with the last of his boxes under his arm. He was moving offices for the hundredth time in the enormous, sprawling corporate campus, and he didn't trust the movers with the most fragile and special of his personal possessions. His commute home was about thirty minutes, and since it was early and a nice day, he stopped into the Drive & Shine to rinse the latest snowstorm off his Buick.

The light turned green, and he proceeded into the guiderails, suppressing the slight panic these car washes always gave him, He put the car in Neutral, took his foot off the brake, and fiddled with the radio, even though he knew it would cut out any minute.

He thought back to the weekend before. He and his friend Tom had gone up to Saratoga for the races. Tom lost twenty-five bucks, the cheap bastard. Fred had gone all-in with his $500 holiday bonus. And also lost.

Fred's mind snapped back to the present as droplets of water splashed the left side of his face. He found the source of the leak: his satellite radio cord, passed through the window, was creating a virtual spout for the high-pressure, soapy water to enter. He fumbled around the window buttons, reached lower, found a lever, and pulled. The trunk in the rear popped open, exposing his boxes of office valuables. What to do?!

Fred panicked. He couldn't exit the car, he'd be soaked. He hoped the next wall of water would slam the trunk shut. It didn't; actually, it did the reverse, the trunk flipped entirely open, exacerbating the issue even further.

Finally, after an eternity, the "Go" light lit up, and he sheepishly drove out of the bay, and put the car in Park to evaluate the damage. It was bad. The framed pictures, college graduation certificates, lamps, glassware—even the gag gift picture of Larry and his seventeen cats—were covered in a rainbow sudsy film. The pictures of the kids, the autographed sports memorabilia, all ruined.

He turned the car out of the driveway, and as much as he would have liked to drive to the nearest bar, he made his way home.

Once there, he meticulously removed each item from his sudsy trunk, toweled it dry, and placed it carefully on the garage floor to dry.

An hour later, Fred's wife entered the house, perplexed.

"Fred, what's going on in the garage?"

"Don't ask, honey. Don't ask."

JUDITH BANNON SNOW

I Once Was Two People, But Now I Am One

A MEMOIR

O nce, many years ago, I suddenly became two people. The funny thing was, I didn't know I was two people until twenty years later. Looking back on it, I used to think I became two people gradually, but now I know it was sudden.

When I was two people, most people didn't know. But my mother did. I think that's why she loathed my now-ex-husband. Why she warned me not to marry him. Why she begged me not to marry him.

Her objections were sound. I was already married, and so was he. Unfortunately, when my first husband and I married, our relationship changed drastically. He exhibited unexpected behaviors, which in hindsight I might have suspected, but didn't. The man was a great thinker and expounded fervently on many subjects, but lacked motivation for anything but talking.

Nor could my first husband do things. I was working full-time and he wasn't. I drove him to interviews. When he got an early morning job, I made him breakfast at three-thirty a.m. to get him up and going. When he needed to bathe, it took me over an hour to get him into the claw-foot bathtub. When he finished bathing, it took me over an hour to get him out. He finally gave up on working and enrolled in graduate school to study philosophy. By then we had a baby, and I was working part-time, taking care of the house, the finances, everything. I couldn't believe how my life had changed.

So I married husband number two. My mother and he despised each other. This was hidden, unspoken, but I knew.

I used to think the mutual loathing was because they were so much alike, but now I know this was not true. They were not alike.

My mother knew him and saw the underbelly. In college he had been called 'Ruthless D,' with good reason. I didn't like him then—had no interest in him at all. But later, when I was in dire straits with husband number one, he was all promises and passion. Number two was efficient to a fault, earning a doctorate in psychology, professing to love my infant son and wanting to raise him as his own. His wife didn't want children, he said. To this day his first wife has neither remarried nor had children. But she and I became good friends and keep in touch.

My father was dead long before I became two people, but my new husband was obsessed with him, even though they had met only once, briefly. Revered and loved by everyone he knew, my father was handsome, quiet and reserved, with a dry Irish wit and a beautiful singing voice. He never wanted to talk about himself and was rarely prodded into doing so. He died at fifty, when I was only twenty-two. Husband number two anticipated his own fiftieth birthday (actually all birthdays after twenty-five) with dread, and was almost ecstatic when he passed that milestone without dying. Ludicrous.

When I became two people, I burned old love letters, old photographs—gave up the things I cherished. My original self was gone, buried among the ashes.

My new husband had demanded it, an excessive and hurtful act that he explained was a result of his passion for me: "I love you so completely that I can't stand to see these photographs of you with someone else."

The deep pain this appeared to cause him seemed, under the circumstances, ridiculous. He continued, "You must burn all the letters from him, I can't tolerate being under the same roof with these reminders of your past."

Everything was black or white, love or hate, life or death. I must say these acts of passion were extremely dramatic, romantic, and strangely flattering. I know now what I did not know then—they were the acts of an extreme narcissist seeking absolute control and domination.

When I became two people, my original self acted as though nothing had changed. I believed I still was one person. I had no reason to think otherwise.

Of course I couldn't tolerate thinking of myself as a submissive wife, who let her husband call the shots. So I believed myself to be a strong person in the throes of a grand passion that promised a magical life full of good things for me and my children, the first of whom had been fathered by husband number one.

But then the first (or really the second) betrayal began only three years into the second marriage. It was his first betrayal that I actually knew for sure, that I could actually prove, that for which I had cold, hard facts. He was a consummate liar—a skill about which he was inordinately proud—certainly the best liar I ever encountered. This betrayal was when I was pregnant with our son, our second child together.

The actual first (unacknowledged) betrayal had occurred when the ex was finishing grad school and I was pregnant with our daughter, my second child. I only felt that betrayal in my gut, but could not tolerate the idea that it might be true.

My original self was the 'authentic' person—the one who went to graduate school, earned a doctorate in physical chemistry, and who studied light and materials at temperatures close to absolute zero.

The second self was the 'wife and mother' who was in a fairytale marriage to a handsome and powerful prince. She loved husband number two unconditionally, never raising her voice, even as she tried to protect her children from the tumult and din she never foresaw, never imagined.

The authentic self loved truth and beauty, loved science. She discovered invisible water droplets that trapped particles of light, droplets that turned the light from pure green to ruby red. Then the authentic person put a tiny amount of red dye in the water and transformed the invisible droplets into tiny lasers that dazzled the eye. She gave an invited talk about the amazing droplets, and a grand old man—a Nobel Laureate—thanked her and praised her work. How could she know she was not one person?

The wife and mother was unaware that she stood a step or two behind the husband in the presence of others. She was unaware that she spoke gingerly at dinner parties. She knew better than to speak of books or films, and certainly, never of the invisible droplets.

The authentic person flew to the Arctic, two hundred miles north of Deadhorse, Alaska, landing on an enormous ice floe that was about two miles long. She went to measure the transmission of laser light in the clear waters of the Beaufort Sea. Cables several feet below the ice floe suspended her laser apparatus.

Against the wishes of the exhausted engineers, she insisted that they continue taking data until after one o'clock in the morning, never knowing when the good luck might end. After a strenuous and exhilarating day and night at thirty degrees below zero, just before the sun set in the early hours of the morning, a channel in the ice floe cracked open—narrow at first, but widening quickly to more than twenty meters. One of the three cables holding her laser apparatus was attached on the near side, the other two on the far side. She had no choice. The laser was on the receding shore, and had to be cut loose. The experiment was over, but fortunately the data collected during the long night were more than sufficient to evaluate the clarity of the Arctic waters for long-range underwater laser communications.

In August, the authentic person took her team of diver-engineers to build an undersea laser range at a remote island jetty in the Bahamas. After a full day's work, in the warm evening they drank seventy-nine cent beers on the sand before returning to the jetty to collect more data until after midnight. Early in the morning, they went to the mess for the last meal of the day—mid-rats, they called it, short for midnight rations. The experiment went on for three weeks, and the data were outstanding. The team demonstrated the feasibility of ultra-high data rate underwater laser communication for the very first time. The field test exceeded expectations, and her sponsors and managers were thrilled.

The authentic person drove an hour to work each day. The husband said "It's all your fault, you know. Every morning you drive in the wrong direction. You drive to the east, while I drive to the west. Of course, it's clear, it's all your fault."

The wife and mother never contradicted the husband, even when he blared his ignorance, even when he was dead wrong.

One day, the wife and mother knew something was dreadfully wrong. She realized that his recently begun, now routine, early Saturday morning trips to the 'library' were wildly implausible for a man who never read a book for pleasure.

Another full-blown, preposterous, almost comical affair had begun. The wife and mother was cast off, distraught, and inconsolable. She wept, she raged, she despaired. The oldest child said "What does it matter? You were always a wimpy housewife anyway."

The wife and mother reacted with shock and disbelief. For after twenty years, she had no idea that she had been two people. Now one of them could clearly be discarded.

Her mother might have told her, "At last, you are free. Now you can be yourself again."

RAE STUDHOLME

The Day the Dog Died

Dog Day Afternoon. Dog Park. Is that your dog? This car's a dog. She's a dog. Doggone it! Like a dog in heat. Dogging it. Dog tags. A dog is man's best friend. Seeing eye dog. Therapy dog. Doggie style. Doggerel. Doggedly. Three Dog Night. Rescue dog. Dog Whisperer. Hair of the dog. Dog pound. Dog catcher. Dog biscuit. Going to the dogs. In the dog house. Dogged by it.

The day the dog died, we fed her rare sirloin, the pieces so small that when we fed her by hand, some slipped through our fingers.

The day the dog died, she could barely lift her head. But she still wagged her tail when you suggested a ride in the car.

The day the dog died, it was hot. Humid. The drive to the veterinarian wasn't long enough for the car's air conditioning to chill our broken hearts. Or stop her panting.

The day the dog died, she jumped out of the car before you could fasten her lead. She didn't know she was jumping for the last time.

The day the dog died, you wept. You'd felt guilty because you'd encouraged her to jump off the dock.

The day the dog died, I knew for sure you no longer loved me. We drove to Rhode Island, to East Beach. The empty collar and leash on the back seat. Silent. We didn't see the red flag warning. The waves crashed into me. You looked away as I went under, the day the dog died.

MICHAEL J. GORDON

The Italian Brothers

Immediately after graduating with a bachelor's degree in Art from Temple University, Susan's first job was designing album covers for a music publisher in Philadelphia. The company's offices were downtown, what locals call Center City.

She worked there for three years, often spending lunch breaks strolling through Freeman's, a major auction house only about a block away. Articles in the venerable firm's showroom were available for inspection every day, and a "public sale," as they called it, would be held every other Wednesday. Although hardly anything there would fit her taste or budget—most items could be lumped under one category, late baronial—she enjoyed looking at the paintings and sculpture. For her, it was an ever-changing, free art gallery.

Freeman's sales were the place to go, she decided, if you had a mansion or castle in need of refurnishing. Susan and her husband, Jonathan, had no such abode—they could barely afford the mortgage on their recently-purchased small split-level house just outside the city.

Country auctions were another story, both in style and content, and the further out into farm country the lower the prices were likely to be. The couple enjoyed going to such sales. The fact that they had almost none of what the economists call 'disposable income'—the costs of housing, food, taxes, and a baby saw to that—did not deter them. It was good entertainment, and hope always flickered that the auctioneer would forget about a box of stuff under one of the tables, and give it to them for fifty cents when it was brought to his attention after the event.

One such auction was scheduled for mid-week, when Jonathan couldn't go, so Susan (who worked at home) buckled their toddler, Ben, into his car seat, picked up her friend Evelyn, and went in search of the sale somewhere in the far northern reaches of Montgomery County. Her budget was fifty dollars, and that was stretching it.

They found the event already under way in a barn. Upon the instructions of his brother and only heir, the estate of an elderly man who had lived all his life in the 1870's farmhouse next door was being auctioned off. The decedent had apparently been a confirmed bachelor, but not the archetype who stayed home and stashed away every newspaper and magazine that found its way into his mailbox. This one had traveled widely, frequently to Europe, and saved every souvenir and tchotchke he had bought on each one of those trips.

Having read this information in the auction notice, Susan's interest was piqued. When they arrived, the auctioneer was almost finished selling the farm equipment. Since neither woman was in the market for a hay bailer, harrow, or chicken-plucking machine, they wandered around looking for whatever else might catch their eyes.

Within half an hour, the sale moved on to the contents of the house. Most of the furniture was from the 1950s, worn out, and not worth reupholstering or repair. Attempting to add a little cachet to things not old enough to be bona fide antiques, the auctioneer kept calling it mid-century modern. A few items did look as if they might have been original to the nearly hundred-fifty-year-old house: a pie safe, a sugar cabinet, and a candle box; a trestle table and chairs which had never been refinished; and an unusual cherry wood and maple rocking chair. As a favor to the antique dealers and pickers who were regular customers, these items were brought up first.

Once those were sold, most of the dealers and pickers packed up and left. One by one, the auctioneer's assistants paraded the rest of the items in front of the audience for its perusal. The paintings, Susan knew from her art history classes in college, were worthless. Only one looked good, and then only from far away; a closer look screamed "fake." Even the frames were junk. A small silhouette in an oval frame might have been a genuine antique. She bid up to twenty dollars and then dropped out. It went to a dealer for thirty-five. He'd probably put it on display in his shop for a hundred and fifty. The high price would give him plenty of room to bargain.

The two women and the toddler went outside and ate lunch from a picnic basket on the grass. Susan changed Ben's diaper in the car, while Evelyn went back inside.

"Anything good?" Susan asked when she returned.

"Not a thing," Evelyn answered. Glancing at Ben, who was quietly playing with some toys Susan brought along, she added, "Think we ought to go?"

"Let's give it another fifteen minutes," Susan said.

Ten minutes passed before she started to sweat, and quiver all over.

Evelyn asked, "Are you all right?"

Susan nodded, and pointed straight ahead with her chin. "Look at that!" she whispered. "Do you see what's coming up next?"

It must have been hidden among other things, or in a box, because Susan hadn't noticed it anywhere among the auction items before. But leaning against the table was a glazed terra cotta wall roundel, blue and white, about two feet across.

"The paintings were junk, but that looks like a della Robbia! It must be over five hundred years old!" she whispered.

"Are you sure?"

Still shaking, Susan nodded and said, "I wrote a paper on him in college!"

She didn't have time to go up front and examine it, because just then the hammer came down on the previous item, and the auctioneer quickly announced the roundel. A della Robbia plaque that size had to be worth at least a half-million dollars, maybe more. Susan quickly looked around for anyone who might be an art dealer, but couldn't tell. What did an art dealer look like, anyway?

As the auctioneer's assistant held it up, she could see the roundel a little better. "Don't drop it!" she wanted to shout. Her eyes watered at the sight of the white on blue figures, a group of seraphim hovering over God on His throne, branches with leaves and blossoms and fruit circling the rim. She knew from her studies that Luca della Robbia used a secret, tin-based glaze he had developed himself. He'd taught the process only to his nephew, Andrea, who passed the formula on to his son, Giovanni. When Giovanni died in 1529, the secret went with him.

Steadying herself, Susan raised her hand and said, "Five dollars."

There was silence for a moment. Then a man's voice: "Ten."

"Twenty," Susan heard herself say.

Another silence. "Forty."

She gulped. All she had in her pocketbook, all she and Jonathan could afford, was a single bill with an engraving of President Ulysses S. Grant.

"Fifty," she said.

Again, silence. Except this time, it was broken by the auctioneer saying, "Going once, going twice, SOLD to the lady with the little boy!"

Susan couldn't believe it. For fifty dollars, she had just bought a della Robbia roundel worth a fortune. She and Jonathan could pay off their mortgage! And Ben's college education!

She was feeling light-headed as she walked up to the cashier, and, hands shaking, gave her the money.

Carefully taking the plaque back to her seat, she began to examine it carefully. Hesitatingly, she ran her fingers over the sculpted, deep *bas relief* figures. It was the first time she had ever dared touch such a work of art. She looked at the finish, the craquelure in the glaze. "Well, it should be like that, after more than five hundred years!" she thought.

Turning it over to look at the back, she saw something else—three faded words written in the glaze. She squinted to better focus on the expected appellation, "Luca della Robbia."

But no! Blood rushed out of her brain, and her face fell. She felt faint. Instead of the three little words under the glaze confirming the name of the Renaissance artist, they read, "Made in Italy."

"Made in Italy?" And in English, not even Italian? The thing was a fake! Who would have written "Made in Italy" in 1450?

Thoroughly deflated, and out fifty dollars she and Jonathan couldn't really afford, Susan took the plaque back up to the auctioneer. When he was done selling the ten-inch ceramic souvenir of the Eiffel Tower he had on the block, he turned to her.

"Yes, little lady?"

She nervously told him about mistaking the plaque for a genuine della Robbia, and pleaded to let her return it. Her heart was pounding; She and Jonathan didn't have money to throw away on worthless nothings.

He laughed, and said to the audience, "Whaddya think, folks? The little lady thought this plaque was a real della Robbia! Should we put it up again?"

Suddenly, there was movement in the crowd, and a tall, skinny man in his sixties, wearing a work coat and overalls, came hurrying up to the podium.

"Wait just a minute," he bellowed. It was the man who had commissioned the auction of his brother's estate, and he was in a huff.

"That lady don't know what she's talkin' about! This here plaque is real, a real della Robbia. My brother bought it when he was in Europe. It was made by two Eye-talian boys, named Della and Robbia!"

Susan's jaw dropped, but the auctioneer kept his flapping.

"Whaddya say, folks, what am I bid for this terra cotta plaque? No matter who made it, now it's famous!"

Two or three people bid, and this time it went for sixty dollars, ten dollars more than what Susan paid for it the first time.

She thanked the auctioneer profusely as the cashier refunded her money, and sheepishly walked toward the exit with Evelyn and Ben. In the meantime, the man who had bought the plaque for sixty dollars went up to pay. Taking the roundel in his hands, he looked at it and yelled to the auctioneer, "Hey, what kind of stuff are you selling here? I don't want this thing! The glaze is all full of cracks!"

As they got into the car to leave, the auctioneer was laughingly putting the plaque up for yet a third attempt to sell it to someone who wouldn't bring it back.

Susan wondered whether he'd get a hundred dollars for it this time. She'd gotten a good education.

ISABELLE DOUGLAS SEGGERMAN

Grief

This is not what was anticipated. It's not like the great rogue wave that unexpectedly appears from nowhere on a calm lake. It comes in like the foam of an ocean wave washing onto the shore.

It's not like a little catboat on the bay, battling large whitecaps as they sweep over her bow, nor is it like tacking into the wind on the high seas with the craft tilted at a forty-five degree angle between the water and the sky. It is very much like searching heaven and ocean—and remembering as little jolts of thunder rumble across land and sea.

The lone chipmunk visitor bears no name this year. The smells and beckoning of the fishmonger go unanswered. The two kayak racks on the car roof remain empty. There are no guessing games about the temperature of the pool water.

The Panama straw hats on the coat hooks remain vacant, as will the olive green wool Austrian ones come this fall. The hounds have become lethargic. The gatekeeper moves slowly, although the full heat of the summer has not arrived.

Lightning strikes at random like the quick flick of the sword, inflicting pain instantly then subsiding. The beach is not walked upon. Nor does the salt water chill the feet. The rain comes in the form of tears. Miraculously, the sun rises.

The ashes remain earthbound. Grief has come, playing the game out at its own pace, on its own terms.

When the time is right to say "Farewell," the first spring shower may come gently. The smell of summer's sweet lavender may fill the air. The swans may be heading upriver to find sanctuary in the northern estuaries.

Then, and only then, will it be time to say "Godspeed" as your ashes are scattered upon the water among the waves. For present moments, days and nights, I shall grieve for you, my beloved.

JAMES E. McKIE, JR.

Surprise and Survival

A MEMOIR

The long-awaited rain finally made its debut the last week of July 1955. It brought with it sighs of relief in the rural town of Oxford, Massachusetts. June and the first half of July had been brutally hot and dry that year, and everyone, especially the farmers, hoped the drought was finally over.

Sixty-five-year-old Jack Mellom, a retired machinist, and his sixty-three-year-old wife Albina, nicknamed Bina, were as happy as their farm neighbors. The rain gave the Melloms hope that their parched vegetable and flower gardens might be rejuvenated. Looking out of his rain-spattered kitchen window that morning, Jack did a little soft shoe dance and invited Bina to join him. As lean, six-foot Jack and plump, four-foot-ten-inch Bina danced, their mismatched anatomies made a comically touching sight.

Actually, they were doing what they called their "rain dance" not only to celebrate the precipitation, but also to entertain a small audience. Their three grandchildren seated at the kitchen table—eight-year-old Rita, twelve-year-old Jackie, and fourteen-year-old Jimmie—looked up from their cereal bowls. They were in stitches, laughing at their string bean Grandpa and their chubby little Grandma. Jack loved hamming it up for the grandkids and had a barrel full of jokes, stunts and stories that never failed to delight the children. Every summer since Jack and Bina bought the old mill house in 1947, they had enjoyed the summer vacation company of these three children.

Now, in 1955, they and the children were about to experience a strange summer of extremes. When the grandchildren arrived for their usual two-month vacation on July first, they quickly noticed patches of dead grass on the lawn. Their grandparents' flower gardens looked stunted, as did the large vegetable garden. Grandpa explained that the town was rationing water because of a rare drought. It hadn't rained in over a month, and the water level in the reservoirs was getting dangerously low. But children being children, they began their annual sojourn having as good a time as ever.

During the last week in July, a light rain finally brought a little relief, and the hope that bone-dry lawns and gardens would rebound. It also brought laughs as the grandparents did their rain dance. Happily, it rained every day that week and the drought was declared over. After another week of rain, Jack and Bina ceased their rain dance, as New Englanders started wishing to see the sun a little. They rationalized that, now at least, the reservoirs' water levels were beginning to return to normal. No one had an inkling that August was to become the month of the monsoon.

In New York City, June and July had also been brutally hot. On August first, Jim and Irene escaped for their annual four-week vacation. Jim loaded their 1932 Chevy sedan with the suitcases and drove the nearly two-hundred miles to Oxford via the Hutchinson River, Merritt and Wilbur Cross Parkways. If it were up to him, it would've been a non-stop drive, except neither Irene nor the Chevy thought that that was a good idea. While the station attendant gave the old car a big drink of thirty-cents-a-gallon low-test gasoline, Irene visited the grimy toilet. Heavy traffic and bad weather caused the trip to take nearly five hours. It rained intermittently the entire time.

The kids were excited to see their parents, but disappointed because this meant that their vacation was half over. Because of the lateness of their arrival, Jack and Bina were extra happy to see their daughter and son-in-law safe and sound. They also were glad to see the couple because the daily rains meant that the kids would continue to be cooped up in the house day after day. Jack and Bina worried that the children, good as they usually were, might become a handful for them. Neither one mentioned this concern, lest it be taken the wrong way.

The rains continued. Just when it appeared that a break in the weather was a week away, a tropical storm named Connie skirted the coast on August 11-13th, dumping four to six inches of rain on Connecticut and southern Massachusetts. Then, when it seemed the weather couldn't get worse, it did. A week later, second tropical storm, Diane, tracking a path similar to Connie, but much closer to the coast, deluged the already saturated ground of southern New England with thirteen to twenty added inches of rain. This was the straw that broke the camel's back, causing a once-in-a-century flood. Smaller rivers and streams topped their banks, and became raging monsters, swallowing anything in their path. Small reservoir dams failed, releasing tidal waves of water, mud, and debris on valleys below.

Situated on the west end of Depot Road, where it terminated at State Route 12, the Mellom house was one of two houses no more than twelve feet above the small French River. The river was on the opposite side, and closely parallel to the highway. Jack and Bina's mill house was set back from the river only by about a hundred yards.

About four a.m. on August 18th, sirens awoke everyone in the Mellom house. Upon awakening, Jack realized that the house had lost its electricity and water when he couldn't turn on the lights or flush the toilet. He and his son-in-law used a flashlight and retrieved a canvas wading pool from the house's dirt floor basement. They placed it outside under the roof gutter downspout to begin storing water. Irene helped the kids get dressed quickly, while Bina went downstairs to try preparing some breakfast.

Jack told his son-in-law that he had been awakened earlier, about two a.m., by a strange noise. The house still had electricity then, because he remembered turning on the hall light and going downstairs to the front porch. Outside, despite the wind's howling, he could clearly hear the same odd noise. It seemed to be coming from the river. He described it as a horrible, low grinding noise, accompanied by thumps that he could both hear and feel.

After a breakfast of leftover hard-boiled eggs, day-old crullers, and warm root beer, the two men took a quick hike down to the river. They couldn't get close because the small river was now five times its usual width, a raging torrent that looked like movies they had seen of the Colorado River rapids. Its color was that of coffee ice cream, and tree branches and house parts were flying by at an incredible speed. Every once in awhile, they also saw undermined riverbanks toppling into the widening river and being swept away.

Jim remembered Jack having to shout over the roaring background sounds and giving up in favor of an arm gesture that said,

"Let's get the hell out of here."

Walking back to the house, Jack said that the most amazing thing of all was the disappearance of the entire milldam. Constructed of enormous quarried blocks of granite, and thirty feet wide by twenty feet high by ten feet thick, it had been swept away. The large millpond behind it, where he sometimes fished with the boys, was also gone. He kept muttering, over and over,

"I can't believe that dam is gone."

Soon after coming back to the house, a new siren got everyone's attention. It was an Oxford fire truck, slowly rolling along Depot Road. At intervals, a fireman with a bullhorn announced that all of the houses on this lower section of the road were to be evacuated as soon as possible. Residents were directed to seek higher ground until further notice, and to take extra clothing, rain gear, blankets, medicines, and pets. They were also told that they could expect to spend a night or two away, until it was determined safe to return home.

Before the truck could get away, Jack walked alongside and

asked what the specific danger was that they faced. The fireman said there was a real chance that a very large dam up river was going to fail, and the houses on lower Depot Road were in great danger if that happened. Jack rejoined the family and got things moving fast.

Within half an hour, they had collected all the necessary items, including the Melloms' little one-eyed mutt. They walked up the hill behind the house to a small road that paralleled theirs, and turned right, then left, uphill along a steep, unpaved fire road. Although the weather gods had mercifully stopped the rain, that pathway was now like a streambed. After about a quarter mile they saw a small group of people sitting on blankets in an open area. The people waved and invited the newcomers to join them. Other neighbors subsequently joined the group. The evacuees' makeshift encampment numbered about thirty people.

Sitting down on his blanket, teenager Jimmy was both excited and terrified by the day's happenings. The campsite, if you could call it that, was several hundred feet higher than his grandparents' property. From this high vantage point, he could look far down to the roof of their house and beyond, over ranges of hills that stretched to the Massachusetts-Connecticut line.

To his right, his siblings were teasing each other as they sat on their blankets. To his left, his grandparents and parents appeared almost like statues as they stared unblinking to the horizon. It seemed to Jimmy that they were in a strange trance. A shiver ran down his back as he wondered what they knew that he didn't. The Melloms' dog, Tippy, was leashed and sat on her doggy blanket. Grandpa had rescued her several years ago from traffic near his employer's company in downtown Worcester. Tippy was panting, and seemed to be concerned about something. But maybe that was just his imagination, the boy thought.

Getting up his courage, he asked his father what was really going on. His father hesitated until Grandpa nodded to tell the teenager. Jim began,

"It's about the Stiles Reservoir Dam, a big one up river."

After hearing about the danger and what would happen if it materialized, Jimmy felt the anxiety in his mind and body abate. His father had answered all his son's questions, as if speaking to another adult. For the first time in his life, Jimmie realized that not knowing something was far more scary than knowing it.

As dusk enveloped the blanket-wrapped refugees, the sky began to clear and the first stars appeared. Nibbling snacks and fighting heavy eyelids, the little kids drifted off to sleep. Not long after, most of the adults did so as well in blankets or sleeping bags.

Sometime around midnight, everyone was awakened by one of the adults who had spotted a bright flash far to the south. Periodically, intense blue-white flashes appeared above the horizon in that direction. Someone speculated that it might be a fireworks plant exploding, but it was actually far worse.

What the hillside refugees were seeing was occurring in the town of Putnam, Connecticut, about fifteen miles away. A huge factory that manufactured powdered magnesium had been flooded, tipping hundreds of barrels of the powder into the river. As soon as the powdered magnesium came in contact with water, it exploded. The explosions, which continued for two days, destroyed the factory and many buildings nearby.

Early the next morning, a siren was sounded. Soon, everyone was standing. Down below, a fire engine came to a stop, and a fireman carrying a bullhorn looked up the hill and announced,

"People, it's safe to return to your homes on Depot Road. The Stiles Dam has held and the engineers have declared that the emergency is over. Also, more good news—power has been restored. So, please be careful on your way down that muddy fire road."

Cheers, hugs and, tears burst out among the people on the hill. Tired, hungry, and dirty, the refugees then packed up their belongings and slowly descended the hill to their homes.

Somehow, the old house on Depot Road seemed different. Perhaps it was because now, not one of the three generations took it for granted.

After warm baths, clean clothes, and a hot breakfast, Jim and Jack took the boys for a walk down near the French River. The devastation they saw along Route 12 made them awestruck. The familiar landscape had vanished. Several riverfront houses were gone, as were two old dams and their millponds. Green Briar, a development close to the river, sat in a newly created pond, with muddy water half way up the sides of all its houses. Just beyond, the angry river was still racing, carrying with it tons upon tons of floating debris.

They continued walking north about a mile to where Clara Barton Road met Route 12. Not a trace of the stone bridge that spanned the French River near the junction remained. In its place was a gorge, perhaps fifty yards across, through which the river pounded.

Standing on the far shore at the edge of the severed road, about twenty people were waving and shouting in an attempt to communicate with people on the shore where the boys, their father, and grandfather stood. Many of these stranded people were young. Jack guessed they probably were summer residents from a camp for diabetic children located up that road. Whatever words they were yelling never made it across the loud river. The messages they were trying to send were swept away with everything else the river took. A state trooper on the scene acknowledged Jack's concern and told him that an emergency evacuation of those stranded people had just been launched.

A week later, when Jimmie and his family returned to New York, he knew that his summer of 1955 had forever changed him. For the first time, he felt older and wiser. He also realized that high school and summer jobs would make it impossible to enjoy the two-month vacations in Oxford anymore. On the bright side, he was growing like a weed and discovering girls. But this summer, in particular, was one he would never forget.

JENNIFER J. FRANCHERE

The Gathering

"**A**re we passing to the left or to the right?"
This question, recently asked at a large family dinner hosted by my mother, nearly felled me from my chair in giggles. I never paid much mind to the level of formality at gatherings on my side of the family, until two things happened. First, I met my husband's savage family. Second, I casually said to my mother, "You know, I really don't stress about cooking, cleaning, and shopping when you come for a visit."

To which she responded, "So I noticed."

Living distant from extended family has its pros and cons. As tightly bonded as my father, mother, brother, and I became, at holiday time we branched out to include four neighbor families as well. As the oldest of ten children, I was plagued by requests to play the "mom" role in games of house and humiliated to still sit at the kids table at age 15. All the neighbor families seemed to play by the same general rules of etiquette as ours, though, and I didn't notice a huge difference from our reunion gatherings with our extended family back in the Midwest. Other than the addition of Betty Goldman's cold, dense stuffing squares, that is.

Someone said grace, with a blessing to the hands who prepared the meal. A card table held all the trimmings, which were then passed politely, one plate at a time around the table. The meal was followed by sweets for the little ones and liqueurs for the grown-ups. Ladies cooked, guys cleaned up, though that last part evolved over the years. I fell asleep to the sound of adult chatter, never quite catching or understanding the topics of conversation, thank goodness.

The neighborhood gathering was in addition to a quieter celebration among the four of us in my immediate family. At some point, a Christmas Eve tradition emerged of setting a table on the floor of the living room in front of the fireplace, getting all dressed up fancy for church, and eating clam chowder and King crab legs on china by candle and firelight. I wonder now if that tradition got started at a time when we were awaiting a furniture delivery. Anyway, it worked for us, and I still long for those quiet, intimate celebrations.

When we traveled to gather with family on holidays, it was always to Sioux Falls, South Dakota. By plane, by car, by train; from the West and from the East. While we moved every four years, Tom and Pat's house was a permanent homestead in my childhood, with its contemporary ranch design, high ceilings, extravagantly carpeted bathroom, and a finished basement with a ping pong table, movies, games, and even a KISS pinball machine. We knew we were "home" when we turned the corner by the HyVee, then left into their driveway, walked through the garage and mudroom, and into welcoming arms in the kitchen. If it was Christmas Eve, a pot of oyster stew was on the stove, and lefse, a favorite Norwegian treat, was on the counter. The formal dining room was set with fine china and silver, dusted and polished for the occasion. Still the kids table for me though.

Merging families and the traditions that go with them is no easy feat, yet all couples manage it, for better or for worse. I was completely appalled at the first Thanksgiving I celebrated with my husband's family. No grace, no side table, and they didn't pass a single plate! It was an uncivilized free-for-all, spoons flying, everyone standing and sitting and grabbing. And they were, and still are, so very loud. I'm completely certain I asked the proper passing question, but wasn't even heard in the din. They have this crazy "the more the merrier" concept for Christmas Eve that also includes random interruptions from unexpected friends and neighbors, all with a wide-open invitation.

Over the last fifteen years, I like to think that my husband's and my family traditions have rubbed off a bit on each other. I grab like everyone else now, but we do say grace, even if it's a stock Catholic prayer. While I may never understand the allure of the pasta, pizzelles, and anginettes, I appreciate the gathering now for the casual, fun madness it is.

The Sioux Falls and neighborhood holiday gatherings are no more. Gone also are the intimate dinners on the floor. New traditions started from their seeds though- I make a kick-ass clam chowder for our quiet Christmas Day celebration.

ISABELLE DOUGLAS SEGGERMAN

A Slow Progression

It started about eight years ago. At first I thought very little about it. Slowly, ever so slowly, it began to take on a life of its own. It is leading down a path of no return, and my only hope is that your journey into the uncharted areas of the mind is not frightening.

You have been in the wine importing business for the past sixty-five years. As a result, you are well known and even revered in some circles. When you traveled to Europe to select wines, you spoke the language of the country, whether it was French, Italian, German, Spanish or Portuguese. Your accent was not a fine one, but those who owned the chateaux as well as the helpers in the vineyards never minded, because you had made the effort, and fortunately had the ability to laugh at yourself.

This endeared you to the owners whose wines you would represent in the U.S. market. Many have been with you for decades. In fact, they seem to admire you more as you age. The Europeans tend to have an appreciation of, and respect for, their elders, unlike many young and fast-tracking Americans.

Your flexibility and spontaneity, intelligence and imagination have allowed you to forge new paths in your spirited life. The Dali bottle you conceived was brilliant. It may have been the first designed by a famous artist. The Brooklyn Bridge commemorative label was another winner. The bottle is now a collectible. I'm not sure its contents are!

When you had an idea or vision, you simply went for it. Life off the cuff can be daunting for many, but never for you.

Fortunately, your wine importing company had a large office staff, as well as a great sales force to back and follow-up for you.

I remember one trip to Cognac. Your mission: to get the best cognac agency. We drove into the center of the small city. You went into a fine wine shop and asked the proprietor what the best product was, firmly stating, "Not the most expensive, but the finest. The one you would drink." With that knowledge, and a good map of the region, your mission began. You phoned ahead and met with Monique and Pascal Fillioux at their chateau. After tasting the amber liquid in the library, you showed your appreciation for their three consecutive generations owned vineyard (the only one in the appellation controlee), and using your rotten French—they found it charming—the Fillioux agency was yours. As chance would have it, they had dismissed their former agent and importer the week before.

You needed an Armagnac to round out your portfolio, so off to Gascony we drove in a little rented Renault. You have never made hotel reservations—most disconcerting, I'm sure, for anyone who might accompany you, but you always found a perfect place. Good hotels often might have had last minute cancellations and would be anxious to fill the room before nightfall, possibly at a negotiated price.

This land had wildness to it, the terrain vast and windswept. It was the land of the Three Musketeers. Your appointment was with a producer whose product you had not yet tasted. Typically, you would not read a road map, simply winging it while contemplating the route at leisure in the middle of a roundabout.

We eventually arrived at some crumbling stone walls. You drove up a long dirt path accompanied by chickens and roosters. We stopped at a hovel, which appeared to be our destination, and were met by a pack of snarling German Shepherd dogs.

We were greeted by a man who looked so much like d'Artagnan, it felt as if we had been transported several centuries back in time. He wore brown, partially laced leather boots, a red scarf around his neck, and a white, open-necked shirt with long, full sleeves that flapped romantically in the breeze. He led us to an orchard where a stone table with a bottle of champagne and crystal glasses awaited. The Musketeer's wife joined us. She was sporting a rhinestone-covered blouse, tight black satin pants, and high heels. She spoke no English, and I no French, but you boys did fine without our input.

Lunch was served in a building with white-washed walls that had seen better days, and an ancient terra cotta tile floor. An old peasant-type woman served us. She then joined us at the table. You flirted outrageously with her, calling her Coco Chanel. We left well fed, with a verbal agreement to represent their product.

We should have tasted more of it. You should have not flirted quite so much, and we should not have allowed them to put us up in a spa-like hotel. It took us about half an hour of driving on dusty, unknown roads to find it. We came upon what looked like a stage set, a mockup of a small European village, one block wide, dumped in the middle of nowhere. We strolled the small main street and dined at some health food restaurant, which seemed to be the only act in town. Then back to the hotel/ spa to retire. Our beds had been turned down and there was a healthful prune, in lieu of chocolates, on each pillow.

Upon arrival home, the charm of the wild and rugged Gascony hills had left us, and we found that the Armagnac did not taste nearly as good as it had while holding a glass of champagne in our hands while you marveled at the sequined top. You decided not to represent them. After several weeks of 4:00 a.m. calls from the Musketeer (perhaps he had forgotten the time difference), it was understood that you were not the right agent for them. I think they resented treating us to the prunes, but you shook it off as the cost of doing business.

One of your strong points was discovering absolutely delicious wines at reasonable prices. You once sold a marvelous Chilean wine. This winery found you. Their wine was way under the money. Your customers loved it. You rapidly sold your entire first container and ordered more. But not only was there no more wine to be had, the entire company had disappeared. It then dawned on you that you had been involved in a cover-up sting operation for the C.I.A.

Bargains have been big with you throughout your life; prudence, not necessarily so much. This trait has extended well beyond your business world. At one point you owned six navy blue blazers. Your justification was that they had been on sale! A year ago you, started to buy art at auction. This was an expensive endeavor.

My forté has always been the dead and well listed European artists. A Modernist, garishly colored painting was one of your first buys. This purchase made no sense whatsoever, even if it was a "bargain." The auction houses and I quietly and discreetly cut you off.

Your always casual style has become more so over these last few years. You have always sealed a deal with a handshake. This worked well in the smaller, more intimate world of wine in the old days. Now, however, the world is being flushed with alcoholic grape juice from every part of the globe. More rich romantics and entrepreneurs than ever are going into the business. There is more competition all around, and only so much wine that can be drunk.

Small wineries have been unable to keep up with the cost of modernization. Their children have gone to the cities to find more lucrative work. Large conglomerates have gobbled up the fine little vineyards. Your former employees have either retired, changed careers (romance doesn't always pay a child's tuition), or started their own companies.

It is those people who have done the most harm to you as you have aged. They have come calling, flattering and cajoling you into sharing your agencies. Per your usual style, nothing has been done with a written contract. As a result, the unscrupulous have simply walked away with many of your producers and their products, most of which you have made name brands, and big sellers.

Patience for you has never been a virtue; it has been an impossibility! Often you would be on chapter three of a novel, while your companion reading at the same time would be on page three. Your mind has flown over the years, and you have come up with some brilliant ideas. In the old days, you had a full office staff and hardworking sales force to bring them to fruition.

But there is no office staff, no sales force any longer. When you sold your company in a leveraged buyout, you signed a non-compete clause. After three years, you re-entered the business as a broker and selector of fine wine. This worked well for a long time, because you had a stellar reputation and the Europeans you worked with found a wise father in you.

As you have aged, however, the boring and mundane have been neglected. A few years ago, you forgot to pay your long-time Spanish partner for a shipment of sherry. Then simple bills, like house insurance, fuel, and phone piled up on your desk. When late fees began to accumulate, I secretly took over the task.

It was February 4th two years ago that the terrain you traveled changed dramatically. You left at noon to go to Trader Joe's in West Hartford, about half an hour away, to buy some treats.

Although we'd had one snow fall after another that winter, the roads were clear, and the sun was shining. Snow drifts forming mounds of dirty ice covered the landscape. The trees were bare, devoid of any color. They looked like dark and evil shadows. The white clapboard New England houses looked as bleak and gray as the land.

By 2:30 p.m., you had not returned, so I assumed that you had snuck off to Nordstrom's to buy another blue blazer. By 4:00 o'clock, I was getting worried but decided to sit by the phone in case you called with what I hoped would be a good explanation. The phone jingled. I answered and practically hung up the phone on the caller, as I wanted to keep the line clear. At 5:00

p.m., I was beginning to panic and was also pissed, because it was time for our evening bottle of wine. Refusing to accept any calls, I made one at 6:00 to your lawyer. I misdialed and reached your former accountant by mistake.

"Bill, I am extremely worried about my husband. Should I call the state troopers? I don't want to make a false alarm, or be labeled an hysterical old woman."

Bill's response was brief: "Call the police."

Two troopers came to the house within ten minutes. They asked where you might have gone. I said, "Trader Joe's, and perhaps Nordstrom's…unless he got a one-way ticket to Paris."

My daughter called to check in from her home in New York City. She said, "You don't tell the law enforcement that your husband has gone to France without you!" The two men separated. Detective Milardo stayed in the dining room with me and got details: your social security number, your credit card numbers, make and model of your car, a physical description, including any distinguishing body marks. I gave him a full description of what you were wearing, from your gray wool quilted Burberry jacket down to your blue striped Brooks Brothers boxers. The other detective was still in the living room, I assume looking for blood splatters behind the sofa.

Twenty minutes later, my daughter called again. She said that she'd had the surveillance cameras checked at Trader Joe's, where you did appear, and at Nordstrom's, where you did not appear. It saved the troopers time, so they concentrated on alerting the credit card companies in order to find a paper trail you might have left.

Discovering no gore in other parts of the house (granted, he was subtle about the search), the second trooper rejoined us. They requested a recent photo of you. The one at hand was a very flattering one in which you were standing pouring wine and wearing a navy blazer. I began to feel as if I were watching a movie, not one of the participants in the scene at all. They announced that they would put out a "Silver Alert," which means that an older person has gone missing. At the time, I had no idea that your photo would be broadcast on all of the local news channels throughout the Northeast.

As they were leaving, there was a knock at the door. I thought, "Thank God it's you, and you better damn well have a good explanation!" It wasn't you. It was my close friend, Marge DeBold, our former town selectman and a sound and credible person. My daughter had called her and said "She was worried about me." Marge came over immediately.

Since she was blocking the troopers' cars (yes, with the flashing blue and red lights still going), she went out with them to move hers. I think it might have been at that time that the police asked her about you and me. She told them that we were devoted to each other. My statement about a plane ticket to Paris bothered them.

Marge and I then sat with the dogs at our feet, waiting. At ten p.m., I tried to nuke some frozen homemade pea soup for our supper. I could not get it to thaw and was getting more and more upset. At 10:30, my daughter called and said she was coming up. "No, please don't do that. You don't have a car. There is nothing you can do, and it's not fair to you." "Too late, Mom, I'm pulling into your driveway now, so please open the door."

The three of us sat and waited. The soup still wouldn't unfreeze. No one was hungry. I kept murmuring to myself "think, think" where could you have gone. It was now 1:30 a.m.; I handed Marge a toothbrush, and the three of us decided to get some rest. The phone rang. It was the chief of police from Windsor, saying you were safely with him. I said we would be there in half an hour. He then said, "I am in Massachusetts, not Connecticut." Where the bloody hell was this Windsor? My daughter took over the phone and got directions. You were about three hours away. The chief said he would stay with you at the station until we arrived. He said you were, "a little disoriented, and just wanted to go home to Haddam."

Since the area code of the station was the same as my

brother's, I called him and got him out of bed. His wife made sandwiches for you and a large pot of coffee, and off Puck went in the middle of the night to stay with you until our arrival.

We took my daughter's borrowed SUV. I grabbed a bottle of French rosé to give to the chief. There really wasn't much in the way of another thank you present in our house to offer. The three of us headed north by northwest. It took about three and quarter hours. We passed through Springfield, and Northampton. The roads were clear, the moon shining, and the snow-covered landscape could have been anywhere in New England.

We arrived at the station. You were fine, although you did not seem to realize where you were. The police chief looked absolutely exhausted. My brother was drinking a cup of coffee. I asked the chief "whether he drank," simply wanting to give him the bottle of wine with me as a "thank you." It was later pointed out that one never asks law enforcement "if they drink," especially while on duty.

Now it was time for our return trips. However, all the cars were very low on gas, with your meter pointing close to empty. It was 4:00 o'clock in the morning, but my sibling knew of a gas station that would be open. With Puck in the lead, our caravan followed. The station was closed. No problem, there was another in Pittsfield. I was afraid that your car could not run on fumes much longer, but my brother said, "not to worry; it was all downhill from here." After tanking up the three vehicles, courtesy of my Visa card, we went our separate ways, Puck home to Sheffield, you and my daughter in the SUV and Marge and I in your car back to Connecticut.

We passed the Smithies in Northampton as their dorm lights were slowly coming on, and crossed the border as dawn was breaking. The sky was a soft pink and quite beautiful. We were too early for commuter traffic, so the trip was pleasant and the feeling of relief even better. Marge went home. You went to bed, and my daughter and I just sat at the kitchen table, exhausted and grateful.

Then the phone calls came. Your nephew from Manchester, Massachusetts called to say that he had seen your picture on television the previous night. At first I thought he was talking about some wine program you had done. That was not the case; he had seen the Silver Alert. The accountant, Bill, called to check. Your lawyer, who was on a skiing trip but had been alerted by Bill, called. An old friend from Glastonbury phoned. He dodged around the subject for a few seconds, and then said, "Let's call a spade a spade. What the hell happened to your husband?" Apparently, half of Haddam was watching the television last night, although very few mentioned that to us at the time.

Then the credit card company called and said that there had been some unusual activity on the card last night. I told them not to worry, yours had been canceled. The woman at the other end of the line said it was my Visa they were concerned about, not yours, and that that there had been some odd transactions on mine last night. She said that my card showed three stops for gasoline within five minutes of each other. I explained that it had been a long night, and that the charges were all right.

By the time Detective Milardo came back to check at noon, you had been up for a few hours and were gloating about how you were now a television star. I got so mad that I said that the broadcast photo showed you in your bathing suit with a beer in your hand, and that all told it was an ugly picture of a wine importer. Thankfully, that hushed you. Gently and ever so nicely, the detective asked to see your license, and asked you to give it to him to keep until you took another driving test, which was protocol in Silver Alert cases. To this day, we remain a one driver household.

For years, you have been a connoisseur of fine foods as well as wine. Crème Catalan was a favorite in Spain, as well as Manchego cheese, and baby lamb chops grilled over grape vines. Chocolate mousse was at the top of your list in France, and Dover Sole always was ordered when you were near a cold-water seacoast. You've delighted in eating mussels washed down by a bottle of Muscadet at the Central in Trouville. Your mantra has always been "the best of everything in moderation."

So, now it's a bit surprising that you will grab a one pound bar of 72% dark chocolate late in the afternoon, and eat away until you are reminded that dinner is still to come. The homemade almond cookies are now hidden and doled out on a three per serving basis. The insatiable sweet tooth seems out of character, the lack of restraint almost childlike.

You were once a voracious reader of non-fiction, especially history. You and your brother-in-law would talk at each other, expounding on historical facts with neither one coming out the winner. Several months ago, your reading stopped. The interest was gone. We tried books on tape, which were a success until a few weeks ago when you tired of listening to Tony Blair drone on and on.

You stopped playing duplicate bridge a few years ago. Arranging a game was always a nuisance for you, but the goal was to play and usually win so you were propelled to make phone calls, have clean cards and score sheets ready. Your favorite player died last year. You found those who remained not up to your speed, and the games ceased. Solitaire filled your card hunger for a while. You lost interest in that about six months ago.

Beau and Gus are your great comforts. The spaniel and the Pekinese get a daily stroll from you. When you remember to change their water bowl, you do. When you don't, it seems to get done anyway. If it's not too difficult to get through their coats, you will part their hair so that their monthly Frontline medication can be administered. The Peke likes to cuddle and helps to warm your chilled bones, which seem to be cold even when it's 75 degrees outside.

Life is slowing. Your days begin with breakfast around 9:00 a.m. On a good day, you might read the newspapers, point out sale flyers listing your favorite foods, and perhaps talk about the latest failure of anti-gun control legislation. The dogs are walked.

Then it's back to the house for a doze in the library until lunch is served. With a good appetite you can demolish a can of sardines, an avocado salad, a banana, perhaps a strawberry Greek yogurt, and your new fixation, a Sam Adams Boston lager. You choose not to answer the phone; maybe the buttons on the portable confuse you, so often calls from our few remaining friends are missed. Socially, you are not suffering from overexposure. By 7:00 p.m., after an early dinner, you are ready for bed and generally under the covers by 8:00.

The days go by, sometimes quite fast, other times dismally slowly. You are in your house. You are physically comfortable. Sadly, your eyes reflect and convey your realization that things are not the way they used to be. Those green-brown windows reflect the decline. Hopefully, it is not too painful for you. Chances are that the thought or emotion that clouds your eyes may not linger for long in your mind. You are safe and protected. You are not alone.

JUDITH BANNON SNOW

Seventh Grade

Seventh Grade (Child)

Seventh Grade (Child)
I hate P.E. I hate seventh grade. Nothing is fun in P.E. When I went to Fauntleroy Elementary, I loved recess—no P.E., just recess. We played hopscotch, dodge ball, and jumped Double Dutch on the playground. We played "Pony Express" on the dirt part of the playground. Between the old gym and a steep gulley, there is a little bit of playground with a snail game painted on the asphalt. We talked about secret girl things there under the trees.

In P.E. class we have to wear stiff white shirts and ugly shorts. The lights are too bright and there aren't any windows. We're all lined up in rows on the cold floor. I am always cold in gym class. After that, the worst part comes. We have to undress for showers even though we aren't dirty or sweaty. I am embarrassed in my white undershirt. All the other seventh grade girls have bras.

My mother doesn't know that, even if I don't need a bra, I NEED A BRA! And I'm embarrassed to ask her for one. I'm embarrassed every day in the locker room. I hate seventh grade.

Seventh Grade (Adult)

Seventh grade marked a turning point for me—everything changed for the worse. I had always loved school. Fall was my favorite season and the first day of school was my favorite day of the year, more anticipated than Christmas, Thanksgiving, Easter, and the Fourth of July. The shock of junior high was aesthetic, as much as anything. I had always loved Fauntleroy, my grade school. I even loved the name, especially when compared with the less-than-mellifluous David T. Denney Junior High School. Fauntleroy was an old brick building with a pleasing façade. The classrooms were inviting, with tall elegant windows, and old burnished wood desks complete with flip-up seats and real inkwells. The auditorium, which doubled as a cozy lunchroom, had a raised stage with maroon velvet curtains. I performed on that stage—I was the princess in "The Princess and the Jam-Jam" and the angel in the Christmas pageant.

Denney Junior High was alienating, with its sprawling maze of modern structures, including a half dozen slipshod, detached portable buildings. As a child I had looked forward to taking English and History, but instead ended up with Language Arts and Social Studies. These classes, located in one of the portables, were combined into one grueling two-period class at the end of the day. Our teacher, Mr. Busch, wrote his name each day on the blackboard in a rounded, feminine cursive hand. As he wrote, he sounded out the letters: B-U-S-C-H, as though to be reminded of his own name. The class was completely out of control, two unrelenting hours of spit wads, paper airplanes, and riotous 12-year old boys. Seated at his desk, the dejected, trembling, middle-aged man had no idea what to do. On a good day, we could talk him into letting the class go outside to play baseball.

Ironically, these impromptu baseball games were much more satisfying than anything we did in Physical Education, or P.E., as everybody called it. P.E. tore the heart out of every athletic activity, even team sports like volleyball and basketball. Outdoor activities were ruined as we lined up to hit one golf ball or shoot a single arrow. Even these were better than sitting on the cold gym floor doing uninspiring exercises in our unattractive white cotton shirts and navy shorts.

The locker room was humiliating when after our mandatory showers I had to put on an undershirt while the other seventh-grade girls wore bras. As a child, I could talk with my mother about all kinds of things. Well, almost all.

"How does God know when people are married so he can send children?"

"Ask your mother!" said my second grade Sunday school teacher.

Mom had a rudimentary 'birds and bees' explanation suitable for a seven year old.

"What does Kotex mean?"

"Ask your mother!" retorted my next-door neighbor, who had a big Kotex carton full of trash in the bed of her pickup truck.

I was nine. Mom told me what to expect at puberty.

For reasons I still don't understand, I was too self-conscious to tell my mother such a simple thing—namely, that I needed a bra.

KENT JARRELL

The Value of Life in Ethiopia-1984

A MEMOIR

The famine and civil war brought me, a television reporter, to Ethiopia. On the way from the airport into Addis Ababa, the capital, I was crouched in the back seat of a yellow Mercedes taxi, peering out the side window, when I saw her.

A teenaged girl, by the side of the road. Dirty face, scraggly clothes, and begging. She sat slumped next to an emaciated bush, a desperate look on her face. It was a pretty face, or should have been, like the daughter I would later have back in Washington. The one who would grow up happy to be on the rushed verge of womanhood, excited about high school, the promise of college, driving Dad's BMW, boys, ballet, and all the fun and comforts of affluence.

Not this girl. She was alone, hungry, and ignored. My driver never glanced her way as he sped on. She was gone in a second, but the vision of her face froze into my jet-lagged mind. During the next few weeks in Ethiopia, and even today, I am haunted by her. I wonder how long that girl on the street corner in Addis suffered? Had she even survived?

As I began my in-country reporting, I was told that thousands of children, orphaned by the famine up north, had descended on Addis. The boys simply disappeared into the teeming slums, or were conscripted to serve on one warring side or the other. For the young women, there was a different, more chilling, reality.

"The girl you saw could only have been in the city for a few hours," a local source explained to me on background during a clandestine interview at a dingy hotel. "She would have been scooped up immediately because young girls are in high demand. The soldiers, the police, the government guys are always on the lookout for girls. Not for the right reasons."

That was just one sign of the harshness, horror, and brutality of Ethiopia that year. Three weeks before I came to Africa, during Thanksgiving week, I was sitting in the TV newsroom in Washington, D.C., looking for something to do. Watching reports out of Europe and Africa citing famine conditions, I saw a slow-motion disaster. The spring rains never came and the Ethiopian government's pleas for international aid were all but ignored. The story was big in Europe, but had not broken through yet in the U.S.

This looked like a grand adventure to me. I would get to a continent I had never seen. It might make my bones as a rising star and advance me up the ladder, from a contributor to full time status as a CBS correspondent. First, I had to figure out how to convince my news director why he should agree to foot the bill to get me to Africa and back. And I needed a local hook. Why would American audiences, especially Washington, D.C. viewers, be interested in a catastrophe on the other side of the world? In Africa, of all places?

I started my desk-top research and began with my assigned coverage of Capitol Hill. I hit pay dirt in Representative Frank Wolf, a little-known Republican from suburban Virginia. He rode into office on the same surge that elected Ronald Reagan president. Wolf was a religious conservative, but considered a moderate with a non-partisan ideology. Interested in human rights, he struck up a friendship with the newly converted evangelical Christian, Democrat Representative Tony Hall. Hall said it was morally imperative that Wolf go to Ethiopia. A quick call to Wolf's office got the Congressman's permission for me to tag along on his trip.

My news director said, "That's great, we'll cover flights and expenses. You will be on your own, but Wolf is a Congressman. Stay close to him. He's your protection. But who in the hell is going to pay for a cameraman? We can't afford that."

Back to the phone I went. Much of Wolf's local itinerary in Ethiopia would be coordinated by World Vision, the Christian relief organization. My quick pitch to World Vision: I was an accredited TV correspondent, with network connections, accompanying Wolf on his trip. If they would supply a film crew, I would file a series of reports for broadcast in the U.S. and they could use all the raw footage for their own purposes.

Twenty-four hours later, I was booking my ticket to Africa, and learning from zero about famine, international aid, and the civil war in Ethiopia.

In Northern Ethiopia, I was awakened just before dawn by a low rumble I couldn't identify. I was in a hut where I had slept fitfully on the dirt floor and sensed, more than saw, a lightness beyond the open doorway.

Moving outside, I grabbed a sweater for the early morning chill. Then I saw what the noise was: the combined rustle of thousands and thousands of people, too many to count, crowding up against the fence of the Alamata feeding station run by World Vision and Mother Teresa's missionaries. The new arrivals had come in the middle of the night to lie, unprotected, in a field. I would discover they had walked for miles from their villages, leaving behind barren land, desperate for food and medical care.

With so much need, impossible choices of life and death were made in a split second. There was food to feed 13,000 people a day at subsistence levels, but the migration was growing fast. To me, it was an unending tide of distress. Mothers with infants in arms, older children straggling slightly behind, men and women stooped with age, eyes half shuttered in the bright light, and young men, enduring, but often on the verge of anger. They all were dressed in worn and graying clothing. I could make out t-shirts with faded logos of American and European sports teams or familiar international brands. The green Irish shamrock of the Boston Celtics, the orange crest of Manchester United, the black Nike swoosh, the green alligator of Lacoste, were all splashed on the cast-off surplus apparel ending up far from streets of plenty.

The elderly, and especially the very young in extremis, were suffering from lasting malnutrition, lack of protein, dehydration, or contagious diseases, including meningitis and chickenpox. To deal with this, just two doctors.

Who got saved? Who didn't? That was the job of a volunteer doctor from Holland, who came out of the camp's gate and walked among the crowd, armed only with pieces of white paper. He quickly examined one young boy, patted him on the head, and then apologized to his mother, saying softly, "No, mama, I have to pass you."

The mother and child were expressionless. They remained silent, motionless, as the doctor stepped to the next mother and discovered a son wrapped in a blanket.

"But this one," the doctor said, granting her a white piece of paper, the admission ticket to the camp, which would provide the young boy with an emergency high calorie food product and medical care.

I asked the doctor, "Are you playing God?"

"The bad thing is I have that feeling," he said as he continued walking his rounds of instant assessment. "For sure now, I am going to have to choose and I will make mistakes and I know that and that's a bad thing."

I was humbled by this man, by his presence far from the comforts of his northern European homeland, and by his eloquent, almost Hemingway-like description of the haunting selections he was forced to make.

Survival was elusive, even with the coveted white paper. As high noon approached, the heat from the desiccated grasslands rose and gusts of wind swirled around and through the open tents of the camp. No x-ray machines or surgical equipment were to be found here and few of the rudimentary supplies commonly used in mobile emergency medical clinics deployed in disasters back in the U.S. The tools to fight the effects of famine in the African bush were thermometers, stethoscopes, soiled blood pressure cuffs, food kits, a handful of often-outdated medicines, and metal scales usually seen in markets for weighing food, but used here to judge the chances of survival for infants.

The handful of aid workers was aware of the impossible situation and stoically did what they could despite the long odds.

"I think to see one child, one mother, is a help," said a nurse from the U.S., who had felt compelled to volunteer. "We do what we can do and beyond that, it is out of our hands."

Off in a corner, amidst the bustle of altruistic caregiving, was evidence of the lost fight. Four-month-old Mostafa Kafaei lay dead on the brown dirt ground, swathed in a thin and stained sheet. His mother sat cross legged near his feet, her hands to her forehead in unimaginable grief. She had carried her baby 40 miles from their home, and gotten into the camp, but with no reward.

I stood off to the side. Silent. A witness. Not a participant. Behind me, a few yards away, my camera crew did their work with the practiced detachment of undertakers, capturing the low clicking sounds of a mother's sorrow, and the washed-out colors of the flat plain.

Several other children, and a young man, also watched as a shallow grave was dug behind one of the tents. Mostafa was quickly buried. The ritual of death was fleeting and commonplace in this hastily erected humanitarian camp. The young man, interviewed by the reporter from Washington, raised his hand and dismissed a question about the shocking situation at the camp, "It's nothing new. For you, you come here new. It amazes you. You find it different."

I was lightheaded and nauseous from exhaustion, and all that I had seen and felt. As I sought relief, there was no place to hide, no privacy on this barren stretch of stunted trees and hard ground. I could only walk out several yards from the camp tents and crouch behind a low bush to gag and retch.

My suffering, so acute to me in my brief moments in this camp in Ethiopia, was nothing, nothing at all, in the land of lasting drought and seemingly random death.

The young man, striding up the dusty street in jeans, t-shirt, and scuffed sneakers, was not unusually dressed for war torn Ethiopia. It was the chrome-plated revolver he was excitingly waving around that riveted our attention. He screamed at us, then abruptly turned away to grab an elder of the town by the shoulders. He pulled the man close and pistol whipped him across the face.

I was the youngest and most inexperienced member of a small group of journalists who had just walked into Lalibela, a historical town known for its churches carved from rock. We had been dumped at the end of an airstrip on the outskirts by a plane operated by Médecins Sans Frontières, Doctors Without Borders. Lalibela was the scene of fighting between government troops loyal to Mengistu Haile Mariam, the leader of the Communist military junta, and rebels of the Tigray People's Liberation Front. The rebels had captured and then released several westerners two months before. Since then, there had been no word on what was happening in Lalibela. As reporters hunting for a story, we had hitched a ride on the plane to try to find out the status of the conflict in what was one of the country's holiest towns.

Now we were quickly trying to figure out just who this young man represented. Was he a rebel? Was he the government's local thug reporting to Mengistu? He seemed to be speaking Amharic, the official working language of Ethiopia. One of my fellow reporters, Antero Pietila, the Finnish-born Baltimore Sun Moscow correspondent, was big and burly. Unimpressed by the gun, he played a hunch. Antero pulled out his Moscow press credentials, waved them in the man's face, and demanded he call the capital in Addis Ababa, "They won't like it in Moscow if you shoot me. You better make sure you know what you're doing."

A third reporter, David Lamb of the Los Angeles Times, a well-known and veteran Africa hand, calmly watched the confrontation. I figured it would be best for me to do the same, although my legs were shaking and I was struggling to keep my balance. The quick violence at the mercy of an angry, out of control man with a gun, had thrown me into a state of disbelief. We were just walking down a road under a bright calm cloudless blue sky, and suddenly, in seconds, we were in deep, deep, trouble.

Two other young men, armed with rifles, appeared from an alley. We were led away to a compound and told to sit on the dry and crusted ground under a searing midday sun. My mind raced as sweat dripped off my face. What happens next? Are we prisoners? Will they let us go? Will they just shrug, shoot us, and dump our bodies in the acrid and barren fields on the outskirts of town?

Besides my biting fear, I was also aware that this was the reality for a foreign correspondent operating in a conflict zone. That was the career ticket I needed punched.

I turned to my cameraman, who had only met me a few days before in Addis, after flying in from Italy with his sound man.

"Can you turn on the camera?" I whispered. "Don't pick it up, just turn it on and let it roll."

He looked worried and confused. His English wasn't the best. I flicked my thumb. We did share the common language of television journalism. He turned the camera on with a quick touch. A small piece of black adhesive tape covered and hid the red light above the camera lens that blinked when the video tape was rolling. Standard practice in hostile territory.

At least, I thought, there will be some sort of recorded evidence of what was about to happen.

We sat for a half hour, the guards glancing our way from a shaded corner. We waited in silence. There was not much we had to say to each other. My earlier fear, fed by a boost of adrenaline, had turned to numbness. I had fleeting thoughts of home, my wife, and the life we had in Washington. But I couldn't concentrate and couldn't comprehend what would happen next. I never even took out my reporter's pad to take notes.

Eventually, the young man with the gun returned, his pistol now stuck back in his belt. He motioned for us to get up and pointed outside the compound and down the road where we had come. Then he gestured to the sky and quickly gave us an order in Amharic.

David Lamb, hoping he was getting it right, nodded and said, *"Amesegnalehu."* Thank you, in Amharic.

Under his breath, David turning to me first, and then to the others, whispered, "I think he is saying to go back to the airstrip and leave. Let's get the hell out of here. Don't run. Move slowly. Just walk."

I started to stumble forward, nodding my head humbly in thanks, my eyes on the open gate out of the compound.

As we walked through the town, there was silence and stillness. Alone on the street, we could sense we were being watched from the red earth and stone buildings, luminous in the high-altitude afternoon sun.

My cameraman glanced at me with a question in his eyes. I knew he wanted to lift his camera to his shoulder to get a fuller picture. I quickly shook my head, no. His camera stayed at the bottom of his arm, swaying at knee level as he walked, left to right, scanning to capture as much as he could on tape.

We didn't look back. Just straight ahead to the airstrip, about a half mile away, down a gently sloping hill.

We had a small radio transceiver given to us by the pilots of the plane when they dropped us off a few hours earlier. As we hopped out the side door, the co-pilot had said, "We can't wait. It's too dangerous. We have to go on. Call us. We'll circle back and get you."

Now, as we keyed the radio microphone with a squawk and gave our location, a cloud of dust rolled towards the far end of the runway, followed by faint echoes of a series of pops.

"That's gunfire," said the Baltimore Sun correspondent.

"Yup," I said with false bravado as it quickly occurred to me that the seemingly innocuous noise was really the sound of battle. It was getting closer, coming our way.

Remarkably and much to my relief, one of the pilots replied quickly, "Very good, we are a couple of miles out. This will be quick. Firefight near the airstrip. Landing, not stopping. Run alongside. We'll open the side door."

Against the shadows of faraway hills, the black speck of the plane came into view, the landing light shimmering in the rising waves of radiated heat from the ground. It was a de Havilland Twin Otter with STOL capabilities (Short Takeoff and Landing), a favorite for quickly getting in and out of tight places. The pilots came in on a high approach to stay out of the range of bullets for as long as possible. Right above the end of the strip, they cut power and dropped swiftly. The plane bounced once, twice, and skidded on the packed dirt and sand. A puff of dust from the prop wash ballooned out behind the wings.

As the plane rolled towards us, we started running alongside the strip. First one, then two, and then all of us leaped aboard, grabbing the outstretched hand of a crewmember who hauled us in.

The cameraman, loaded down by his equipment, was last. The second he was in, the turboprop engines roared and accelerated. We picked up speed and began to lift off. As we buckled our seat belts, there were smiles all around. I had seen my first glimpse of war and survived it. The thick sweet smell of aviation fuel was heavy as we made a sweeping rising turn back towards Addis, more than 300 miles to the south.

Two and a half hours later, I was poolside at the Hilton Addis Ababa. Safe, sound, relaxed, and satisfied with myself, sipping a scotch and soda while waiting for the delivery of my order of steak frites. I dozed, and then took a dip in the azure blue water, a hotel treat, but a scarce necessity of life upcountry for those caught in drought and famine.

The incongruity of a war correspondent. The ability to pull a rescue rip cord to escape gunfire, violence, and fright, through an expense account fueled airlift to a secure location of pampered luxury.

JENNIFER J. FRANCHERE

Time Passes

Time passes. Two months since my last surgery. Last, hopefully meaning both "most recent" and "final." Six months since my mastectomy. Ten months since my diagnosis. Time to reflect on the impact of this, the changes to my body, mind, and soul.

I have lost my sense of carefree happiness, of settled contentment. Perhaps not altogether, but certainly diminished. Tarnished. Cloaked by a veil of ever-present unease. In place of a soaring sense of gratitude and peace, I feel tethered to something that won't release me, and unable to reach the heights that before I took for granted. Is this a point in time or only a side effect of medication?

I find satisfaction in regaining control over a calendar, filling it up with Things I Like: vacations, day trips, summer camp, volunteering, and scheduled activities. I move through these moments, and allow the time to flow over me, past me. But I appreciate them less.

I am at war with my body. At once, I am disgusted, annoyed, frustrated, and amazed at my physical changes.

The scars. In one place, a thin, barely noticeable line. In others, angry, thick, red braided tissue. Why is it so different? Will it always be?

The weight. The very schedule I set for our summer creates an impossible upheaval of diet and exercise. My physical wellness is out of control, then back under control, then out of control again. I am making no progress, only doing the best I can. I'm tired.

The nipple. Or lack thereof. What to put in its place? I want to be pretty. But I want to be done.

Nearly all my relationships strengthened or at least remained the same. Only one was significantly altered. It needed an adjustment anyway. The people in my life for the most part exceeded my expectations in all respects. That was the best, or only good, part of this—feeling love and receiving appreciation. Being told I was strong and brave. It mattered to hear those words and to receive that attention.

I've not had any great epiphanies. I do not have any great understanding of why this happened to me. I do not know if I caused it, if I inherited it, or if I am done with it. I do not understand my purpose any more, or any differently, than before. I don't know what I'll be doing next month, next winter, or next year. What scares me is that I felt this way a year ago, and now I understand what can be possible in a year. I fear it down deep, although intellectually I hold it in check.

Today I remembered a moment from last year. I'd received the call about needing a biopsy. I drove home, and as I walked from my car to the house, I straightened my shoulders and thought to myself, "I can get through this. I'm the strongest person I know."

Do I feel that way still? Yes. I permitted cancer to be acknowledged, discovered, and removed from my body. I listened, learned, and made smart decisions. I didn't fight or reject this experience as it happened. I didn't freak out, flip out, or lose my cool. "Ok, this is just what we have to do now," was how I responded to each step of the process.

Yes, it was a process; I suppose it still is, and always will be.

Sometimes I feel a small sense of triumph, but it really is not the gleeful "I'm CANCER FREE!!!" that most would imagine. For months, I trained myself to focus on the next step and keep a steady demeanor through all the waiting. Waiting for test results, waiting for surgeries, waiting to heal. I am now afraid

I have trained myself to stay within a too-narrow emotional range.

"Secure" was the first word I drew in a silly psychic card reading last year. I did not understand. Yes, I felt secure, within my marriage, family, career pause, and with my children.

"Well, maybe you shouldn't," my fortuneteller said.

She was right. Maybe we shouldn't feel secure, not ever. I do miss that feeling though. I wonder if it will ever come back.

JAMES E. McKIE, JR.

Tale of a Migratory Soul

INSPIRED BY AN 1805 JOURNAL
OF SHIPWRIGHT W. NORWOOD

In 1802, fifteen-year-old Nigel Wiggins was wanted for petty theft by the local constables in Plymouth, England. Arrest and jail were just around the corner for the street-savvy runaway. His solution was to leave England for good. His plan was simple—he would stow away on the next ship leaving Plymouth. But his plan was also foolish—he didn't really care what type of ship it was or where it was headed.

Thus, in the wee hours of the morning, he snuck aboard the warship H.M.S. *Hydra* and hid in one of her holds. Hours later, when the winds became favorable, the frigate's anchor was pulled and she was under full sail, bound for Halifax, Nova Scotia.

The hold turned out to be the so-called bread room. In the aft belly of the ship, it was where bread and other comestibles were stored along with barrels of water and beer. If Nigel was careful, he would be well fed for the month-long passage. However, that hold was also frequently visited by the galley and pantry crews. After several close calls nearly led to his discovery, Nigel decided to find another area in which to spend most of his time. It would have to be an area that wasn't visited often, but was also close to the bread room. He settled on the carpenter's storeroom, an infrequently visited site that held lumber for repairs to the ship en route. Among the many items stored there were barrels of nails. Nigel removed the lid on a barrel, emptied its contents into a sack that he hid, and smiled at his cleverness—the empty barrel would serve nicely as a head and its lid would help contain its odorous contents.

Initially, Nigel's street survival skills proved invaluable. He was able to elude detection as he slinked between the two storage areas. However, near the end of his first week of residence in the "Hotel *Hydra*," he made a whopper of a mistake!

Awaking in his makeshift bed in the carpenter's storeroom, Nigel decided to tiptoe to the bread room for some food. He didn't know what time it was since it was always dark down in the hold. Shortly after he entered the bread room, sniffing for a started barrel of dried beef, the door suddenly opened and the blinding light of an oil lamp sent him reeling backward onto the floor. The galley crewman who had come in immediately began yelling for help. Within minutes, seamen poured down the ladders and caught Nigel running back to the storeroom. He was escorted to the sea deck and chained to the mizzen mast. It was one o'clock p.m., on a beautiful, sunny afternoon at sea.

Many of the crew, some without having finished eating, had come up from the mess deck to see what the commotion was about. The Captain left his cabin, and stood silently in front of Wiggins, eyeing him up and down. Glaring sunlight caused Nigel to squint, making him look somewhat sinister.

"So, my unlucky stowaway, what's yer name, and whatever possessed ya to stow away on my ship?"

Nigel was silent. Clothed only in his skivvies, the wretch peered down at his filthy feet. Visibly annoyed, the Captain then said,

"Cat gottcha tongue eh, Squinty? Well, maybe able-bodied seaman Jones can loosen it some fer ya."

With that, a big-boned sailor with a wide, ruddy nose stepped forward. In his right fist he held an ash handle from which hung the nine knotted cords of a cat-o'-nine-tails. He snapped the whip in the air to get Nigel's attention. As this large man advanced toward him, Nigel could feel his bladder suddenly empty down his left leg onto the deck. Some sailors began to laugh at the puddle beneath his feet and mock him.

Suddenly, the captain intervened:

"SILENCE! EVERYONE, BACK TO YER DUTIES—NOW!"

The captain then ordered Nigel to be taken away under guard and made to wash, dress, and be delivered unharmed to the captain's cabin. It was time to get to the bottom of the affair.

"Now, let's start again, I'm Captain Richard Waters, this is my wardroom, and this warship is under my command. So tell me who you are and why you're here."

The cleaned-up fifteen-year-old looked at the officer and replied, "Sir, my name is Nigel Wiggins, Sir. I'm here, sir, because my father died when I was young and me Mum had te remarry. Sir, my stepfather hates me and kicked me out of the house after I finished grade school, so he'd have me Mum all to his self. Sir, he kept forcin' her te have kids. Te this day, I hate him, sir…"

The captain interrupted, "That's enough of the 'sir' this and the 'sir' that. Call me captain! So why did you choose my ship?"

"I guess 'cause I always wanted te see the world an' I hoped yer navy ship was a goin' far away from England, sir, er, I mean, captain, sir."

After a few moments of silence during which Captain Waters looked straight into Nigel's eyes, he asked, "What's yer age, boy?"

Nigel figured this was the right time for a white lie, and replied, "Not sure, I think seventeen, captain."

After a pause, Waters said,

"Nigel, ye're illegally on Crown property. Ye have two options: One, since ye've committed a crime, ye'll be removed from my ship and handed over to the Magistrate's Court at Halifax. Two, ye can volunteer to serve the Royal Navy on my ship for the duration of this mission. All ye need do is sign a paper my first lieutenant will give ye that says, 'for serving three years on this ship, you'll have paid for yer crime.' So, what's it gonna be?"

Nigel instantly replied,

"Number Two, Captain Waters, sir."

He subsequently tested the captain's patience by asking some questions. The teenager learned that the ship's first destination was Halifax and that it would only be there for a week before sailing to the Caribbean to harass ships flying French, Dutch, and Spanish flags. He also found out that, with no sailing experience, his rank was landsman, the lowest rank on board; and that his principal duty was doing whatever he was ordered to do by the cook's mate in the galley.

For the next two weeks across the North Atlantic, the galley's mate made his life a living hell. The mate called him "orphan boy" and made him mop the galley, empty the slop buckets and wash dishes in scalding hot water. Worse than the work, and the long hours, was the servant role Wiggins was forced to play to his "master." The teenager was forced to polish the mate's boots and wash his dirty laundry. Worse yet, Nigel was told to lie and steal for the mate. Such criminal behavior was obviously against navy rules, but no one on the ship would learn what was going on, because the mate had told Wiggins that if he squealed, he would be mysteriously lost at sea.

By the time the *Hydra* docked in Halifax, Nigel had decided that he had no choice but to jump ship. The first two days after landing were spent planning when and how to desert. He had decided to wait until close to departure time; but how to get a pass to go ashore had him stumped. He finally concluded that he would have to steal one, somehow. The cook's mate interrupted his ruminations by telling him that some whiskey for the cook needed to get picked up at a certain tavern near the dock. The mate explained that he was too busy to go pick it up himself, and ordered Nigel to do it instead.

Nigel smiled to himself—He damned well knew what sailor the whiskey was *really* for.

"Orphan boy, here's a pass te be showin' the guard an' a note fer the tavern. Go be pickin' it up now, an' if ye're not back in thirty minutes, the shore patrol'll be huntin' ye down. No one's te know anythin' 'bout this, an' nary a drop's to be missin' from the bottle."

As he headed down the gangplank, Nigel smiled to himself—

the hated mate had made it so easy for him. Not only could he now easily desert, he would do so with the mate's thoughtful gift, a bottle of fine whiskey from the bastard.

After picking up the bottle, Nigel spied a church, St. Paul's Anglican. It was the last place they'd think to look for him, a church within sight of the docks. And look for Wiggins they did, every day without success until the *Hydra* sailed. That might have been the end of it, except, Captain Waters had penned a letter to the British Admiralty offices in England, Nova Scotia, and Bermuda requesting Mr. Wiggins' name be placed on the list of British Navy deserters. Waters gave this sealed letter to the Halifax pilot before the pilot departed the *Hydra*. The letter's envelope instructed the pilot to deliver it to the Commissioner of the H.M. Halifax Dockyard.

Nigel watched the *Hydra* from a fishing ship's dock as she sailed out of Halifax Harbor, and the next chapters in his migratory life began. From 1802 to 1805 he was hired as a mate on various fishing boats, first out of Halifax, then Yarmouth, Nova Scotia and finally Portland, Maine. He had worked his way south, always seeking milder winters, but to no avail.

In March 1805, Nigel made a decision, caused by the wanderlust that had periodically captured his soul since he was a young boy. His nomadic spirit was once again awakened, tempting him to visit his Mum and seek closure in Plymouth. Memories of the mild winters and warm springs of southwest England fed a burning desire to ride the Gulf Stream back to his native land. He began searching for a merchant ship that he could sign on with, a ship that sailed from Portland to England.

At one-hundred-thirty-feet long, the merchant ship *Portlandia* was a large brig. Her cargo was lumber, mostly white pine. She had two masts that carried eight square sails, a spanker sail in the stern, and three jibs at the bow. Fully loaded, her crew of thirty could make up to eight knots under full sail. And, this merchant brig was perfect—her first port of call was Plymouth, England.

Portlandia's next trip to Plymouth was scheduled for the week of May 19th, 1805, only two months away. Clearly, Nigel needed a plan and soon. But, how to put the best face on his three years of fishing experience was the first question.

He decided to begin by talking to local seamen who had sailed on the brig or who knew others that had. Portland's taverns in the dock area turned up several mates who provided him with information about *Portlandia's* master of twenty or so years, Captain Eliphalet Adams. They all agreed that he was tough but fair, set in his ways, and a man of few words.

"Captain E.'s got no hobbies or interests, 'cept fer fishin' (a bell sounded in Nigel's brain), an' he loves doin' that aft, while the brig's at anchor. An', oh yeah, also loves listenin' te fiddlin' " (another bell rang).

A pudgy old man walked onto the dock where the *Portlandia* was tied up. He was headed straight for the gangplank until he noticed a young man sitting and fishing at the end of the dock. Now, there was nothing unusual about this scene, except that, next to the man, sat a violin.

"Watcha' doin' with this beautiful fiddle just a layin' on this scurfy dock?"

Nigel looked up with a most pleasant smile and said,

"Doin' my two most favorite things, sir."

"Pleased te be meetin' ye, I'm Captain Adams, an' if ye wanna tell me more, I'm a listenin'."

"Oh, ye mean 'bout this here fiddle?" Adams nodded.

"Well, I'm originally from Plymouth, England an', in school, I learned how to fiddle some. But after school, I also played a fiddle that I found a floatin' where I was a fishin.' I fixed it up an' started practicin' an' later, when I needed to go a beggin' te help me widowed Mum, it came in mighty handy. Lots o' silver coins was a droppin' in me hat those years."

The captain and the crafty young man had a long conversation on the dock. Adams invited him to come aboard where their conversation continued. Eventually, they talked about the *Portlandia* and her next voyage to England and beyond. At some point, Nigel asked the Captain if there was any way he could become one of his crew, adding that he was awfully eager to visit his Mum in Plymouth.

"If yer willin' te be workin' the galley an' the mess, doin' servin', dish washin', and such, I could sign ya up right now fer our next passage in May. Sure would be nice if you'd fiddle some fer me an' me mates te cheer us, 'specially on gloomy days."

Nigel agreed, signed with a handshake, and thanked the old captain, who he had found to truly have a soft heart.

Portlandia cast off and sailed east for Plymouth in the early morning of May 25th, 1805. Up to his elbows in hot soapy water, Nigel was scrubbing breakfast dishes in the large galley sink when the brig first entered international waters. He was humming a made-up song with imagined lyrics that sang inside his head, "Goin' home to see me Mum, see me Mum, see me Mum; once more we'll be together, be together, be together..." when he suddenly heard yelling and saw seamen running for the ladders that led up to the quarter deck.

Nigel asked the first seaman he saw what was up. Another brig was coming alongside and the crews of the two ships were shouting and waving back and forth. He found out that the other brig was out of Portsmouth, New Hampshire, another merchant ship owned by the same Boston Shipping Company that owned the *Portlandia*. They were sister ships built two years apart. Since both were sailing due east in the Gulf Stream for the British Isles, they agreed to travel together for protection—especially protection from privateers, heavily armed sloops that preyed on unarmed merchant vessels.

The mini convoy of the two ships had sailed, side by side, for the next two hours when a sail far on the horizon was spotted portside. The ship appeared and disappeared in fog banks, each time gaining on *Portlandia* and her sister. Not taking any chances, the captains of the two brigs maintained their heading and kept their ships at full sail. It soon became obvious that the ship chasing them was a frigate, not a privateer. As both brigs began to reduce their speed, the frigate fired a shot over *Portlandia's* bow, and Nigel Wiggins' trip to England was dead in the water.

The frigate was the H.M.S. *Cambrian* and her armed boarding parties soon arrived on the decks of both brigs. On the *Portlandia,* Captain Adams presented his and his crews' papers for inspection by the British lieutenant. While others in the boarding party guarded the assembled crew, the lieutenant reviewed the papers. When a subsequent head count was made, a discrepancy was found—the papers of one man were missing. Nigel was that man and he was soon the subject of questioning. When he could not produce any documentation, the lieutenant looked for Nigel's name on a long list of British Navy deserters and found a listing of interest:

"Wiggins, Nigel; H.M.S. *Hydra*; Halifax, 05 Apr. 1802"

His belongings collected, the disgraced galley mate was taken, under force, aboard the *Cambrian.* Captain Adams got off with a warning to be more diligent when hiring strangers in the future, and the *Portlandia* and her sister were allowed to continue to Plymouth. As the *Cambrian* continued south to Bermuda, Captain John Beresford interrogated Nigel. He now learned why the young man felt he had no choice but to desert his hellish experience. The captain was unimpressed—H.M. Navy rules are the rules, the only rules. The captain didn't know that Nigel was obsessed with returning to Plymouth. The deserter had intentionally left that out of the conversation.

Feeling little sympathy for Nigel, the Captain decided to put him to work, and ordered him to report to the *Cambrian's* boatswain's mate. The mate interviewed Nigel and took the impressed man on as his helper. Over the next twelve days, landsman Wiggins proved to be a good learner and an obedient sailor.

Before dawn on June 7th, 1805, the *Cambrian* arrived before the menacing reef that protected St. George Island, Bermuda. As the sun began to lighten the eastern sky, St. George Island appeared on the horizon. Below deck, Nigel was in his hammock writing by the light of an oil lamp. When he finished, he left a large sealed document addressed to the captain on his bed. He didn't appear for breakfast, which was unusual. The Captain was just about to order signaling for a pilot boat to navigate the *Cambrian* through the reef, when he heard,

"MAN OVERBOARD!"

The crew immediately scrambled to get one of *Cambrian's* small boats launched. Ahead, the jumper swam furiously, approaching the reef. Sharks were circling in the clear water behind him. Four oarsmen climbed down the side and began furiously rowing toward the swimmer. The crew watched in horror as the swimmer, now thrashing, vanished beneath the large waves above the reef. Two oarsmen jumped overboard and dove to find the man. Twice they surfaced with no success; but on the third dive, they found him. He was pulled aboard the small boat, and resuscitation began. The four oarsmen took turns pumping his chest to no avail. Exhausted, they picked up the oars and rowed the lifeless man back to the ship.

His body was brought onto the sea deck. His face was blue and all who knew him whispered,

"It's Nigel."

Captain Beresford ordered one more attempt to bring him back to life, without success. Nigel Wiggins' eyes, still eerily open, were gently closed. He was wrapped up in a white sheet to which lead weights had been attached. Beresford ordered the body committed to the deep without ceremony. This order reflected the captain's feeling of betrayal by a deceitful man.

Later that day, an able bodied seaman in the *Cambrian* crew's berth area found a large envelope lying on Nigel's hammock. It was addressed to the captain, and was delivered to his cabin. Beresford was up on the quarter deck where he gave the wheel to a Bermuda pilot to navigate the *Cambrian* through the reef to safe anchorage. The captain then returned to his cabin and found the envelope. Opening it, he found within a sealed envelope addressed to a Mrs. Mary Wiggins Penington, Plymouth, England. Attached to the envelope was a note:

Captain Beresford,   *07 June 1805*

By the time ye be a readin' dis, likely I'll be drowned. I want ye te be knowin' why I risked everythin' dis mornin'. I never told ye 'bout me Mum when ye was questionin' me. I feel free te be tellin' ye now. She's the reazin fer me jumpin' yer ship dis mornin'. Fer sometime, I've bin a tortured by constant worryin' after her. I've bin needin' to return to Plymuth, hopin' of learnin' what happenin' to her o'er the three years since I was a runnin' away. My questions 'bout her haunt me day an' nite.

I 'pologise fer deseevin' ye an' yer crew. I'm a hopin,' some day, ye can find it in yer heart te forgiv me. Te be sure, yer a good man, so I'm hopin' ye'll be mailin' dis enclosed letter to me Mum—not fer me, but fer her. I also ask if ye'd please be a writin' a note informin' her of me death. If still livin', me Mum'll finally be knowin' what was a happenin' te me an' be gettin' the piece o' mind her innosence is deservin' of.

Nigel Wiggins

A year later in London, Nigel's Mum received his sealed letter and the captain's note. Since Plymouth, it had travelled to several towns in England, finally to the current address of twice-widowed Mrs. Mary Wiggins Penington, who now lived in a workhouse. After that letter arrived and was read to her, others in the workhouse for the poor knew that something miraculous had happened. For the first time in the years since the other residents had met her, the depressed, emotionless woman cried and then smiled. Until the day she left this earth to join Nigel, Mary was at peace with herself and those around her.

ISABELLE DOUGLAS SEGGERMAN

Ode to Beau and Bonsal

You died in my arms two days ago
You died in my arms two years ago
These ancient limbs have held you both
Though the bones fragile, the muscles tired
They comforted, supported
Now they are empty

Your dinner plates remain as vacant as my arms
You were a meat eater
You a vegetarian
You snored, as did you
You ran, you walked
Your bite was worse than your bark
Your bark was worse than your bite
You enjoyed leather, especially Italian calf
Your chewing selective
You liked your collar and leash to match
You liked linen, cords with cuffs, and perfect pleats

You twirled in my arms
I in your embrace
The sun dogs danced in the clouds the days you died

I miss you so
You, four legged
And you, just two
Farewell my spaniel, Beau
Farewell, my husband, Bonsal

My arms are empty
Yet they remain open
Should there ever be another You and You.

JUDITH M. COOKE

Nap Time

"**D**on't bother Nana and PopPop while they're napping," Mom told me.

"I'm just going to show them the picture I drew. I won't bother them," I argued.

Mom put her hands on her hips and said firmly, "Ellie, they've had a busy morning, and they have jet lag. Let them sleep."

Mom didn't know Nana and PopPop like I did. Whenever they came to visit, I would wake up early and go crawl in bed with them. Nana would snuggle me, and PopPop would tell me stories about all the naughty things Daddy did when he was my age. Besides, Nana said they came all the way from Albuquerque to see me. All we had done today was watch Justin's soccer game, and that wasn't so tiring.

So when Mom carried a laundry basket to the basement, I took the picture I'd drawn and tiptoed upstairs to the guest room. I put my ear to the door, but I couldn't hear anything. If I could open the door really quietly, I could see whether or not they were awake. Then, if they were still sleeping, I could take a rest with them. If they were up, I would show them my drawing. PopPop had suggested I draw a picture of the three of us. He would want to see it. Turning the knob oh so slowly, and pushing the door as gently as I could, I peeked in.

PopPop was lying on top of Nana, and they were both wrestling. Justin did that to me once—he sat on top of me in the back yard, rubbing my face on the ground until Daddy heard me crying. Then I realized PopPop was naked. They must have started fighting when they were getting into their PJs. His skin drooped in wrinkly folds off his rear end, which was moving up and down, pounding on Nana. She was squished so flat that her legs were sticking out around him. She was trying to get out from underneath him, but PopPop was bigger and had her pinned to the bed. He was grunting, and she was crying, "Jack… Jack…"

"Get off my Nana," I screamed. "Don't you hurt my Nana."

Faster than I knew he could move, PopPop was off her, standing naked against the far wall, his white hair sticking up on the side. Snatching a pillow from the bed, he held it in front of his dinky.

"Ellie, Honey," Nana said, holding the sheet to her chest. "It's okay. We…."

Grabbing a book from the bedside table, I threw it at PopPop as hard as I could.

"You bully! You meanie! You beat up my Nana!"

"Ellie," he said, but I didn't want to hear it.

"You stay away from my Nana!" I shrieked, hurling the alarm clock, which hit the picture of blue flowers on the wall. The glass shattered and part of the frame fell to the floor.

A hand behind me grabbed my arm. It was Mom.

"Eleanor Francis, what on God's green earth are you…" but her voice trailed off as she spotted Nana and PopPop.

"He was hurting her, Mommy," I cried. "PopPop was beating Nana up."

"Oh…oh no…" Mom said, pulling me out of the guest room and shutting the door. "I'm so sorry," she said to the door.

As Mom pulled me to the back porch, I tried to get her to understand. "You have to help her. He's hurting her," I pleaded, sobbing harder than when Justin had pushed me out of the tree house and broken my arm.

"No, he wasn't," Mom told me. "Calm down, and I'll try to explain."

"But Mom," I said, gasping for air.

"Calm down, Ellie. Calm down," she said, pulling me onto the porch swing next to her.

"I hate him," I said. "I hate PopPop."

"No, Ellie," Mom said. "He wasn't hurting Nana." Then taking a deep breath, she put her arm around me and said, "I wasn't going to have this talk with you for a few years. But you're a big girl – eight years old – I think you're old enough."

Then Mom told me the most terrible things. She used words like "beautiful" and "loving," but I knew the truth. It looked mean and horrible, and there was no way Nana liked it. The worst part, though, was when she told me that Daddies did this to Mommies to make babies grow in their tummies.

"Did Daddy...did you..." I began.

"Well Honey, that's the way we got you and Justin," she said, giving me a tweak on the nose.

For the rest of the week, I was extra nice to Nana, but I wouldn't look at PopPop. He tried to sit by me at dinner and wanted to play cards with me, but I just went to be with my Nana every time. She tried to tell me I had misunderstood and that they loved each other very much. But I would never forgive PopPop. Never.

I was glad when they finally went back to Albuquerque. I felt like crying or yelling every time I saw PopPop. When Daddy got back from driving them to the airport, he joined Mom and me in the kitchen. We were making muffins. Mommy was putting ingredients in the bowl, and I was stirring.

"They get off okay?" Mom asked, giving him a taste of batter off her finger.

"No problems whatsoever," he said. "I think they were ready to get back home."

"We all were," Mom said.

Daddy laughed and gave her a little spank on the bottom.

My stomach got tight, and I felt something hot and prickly in my chest, and I knew I could never love Daddy the same again.

MICHAEL J. GORDON

Laid Back

For quite a while, I've been living with my friend Max. Six nights a week, Max works at a place called Bella's, tending bar.

I call him my friend, and I live in his house, but we really haven't known each other all that long. Actually, I only met him the day he invited me to move in. It was an odd situation. I was down on my luck (I'll spare you the details), and hungry. I probably stunk, too—I'd been sleeping in a barn the past few nights.

Max was in his driveway, tinkering with his car. Since he was the first person I had seen as I walked into town that morning, I went over to ask for a handout. I must have looked pretty forlorn, because he not only offered me food, but asked me if I wanted to eat it inside his house. Afterward, he talked to me, and then, out of the blue, volunteered a place to sleep.

As you can imagine, that was a surprise! Not many people would invite a hungry, homeless stranger to move into their home. But Max did. He lived alone, and I wasn't sure how long he'd let me stay. Turned out we got along well right from the start, and have since become fast friends. He has a big bed for himself—once in a while he brings somebody home from the bar to share it with him—and I sleep on the couch in the living room.

It doesn't bother me; I get my share elsewhere.

Normally, I'll get up before he does—not surprising, since he works so late. When he crawls out of bed, we have breakfast together, usually cereal (he eats a different kind than I do), but sometimes eggs and maybe bacon or sausage.

This is a small town, just big enough to have the bar to attract customers who drive in from other places. Most of the people who live here seem really laid back. Max certainly is. He doesn't care what I do during the day, or while he's at work at night.

Occasionally, I'll go along to the bar with him. His shift doesn't start until suppertime, and his boss doesn't mind as long as Max keeps pouring the drinks and chatting up the customers. Even though I don't work there, I've been around so often with him that people think I'm part of the staff. Sometimes I'll walk through the place like a good will ambassador, going from table to table and shaking hands. Once in a while, a customer will even ask me to sit and share a meal.

Bella's is an interesting place. In the early evening, it's usually filled with people eating supper, often families with kids. Later, when the kids and their parents leave, it's only adults, which means less food and more booze. A couple of nights a week, the clientele is almost all adults right from the start. Those nights there's a lot of drinking, and people coming in alone but leaving with someone else.

The place has a juke box, sometimes a live band, and between the music and the drinkers shouting to hear each other, it can get pretty loud. If I get tired of the noise, or of waiting for Max, I'll go out to the parking lot and take a nap in his car.

When his shift is over, we drive home. He gets ready for bed (with or without a friend). I go out in the yard, nose around, and most nights relieve myself in the bushes. Then I bark at the screen door, he lets me in, pats me on the head, and we both go to sleep.

Tomorrow we'll do the same thing.

Like I said, life here is pretty laid back.

PAULA SPURLIN PAIGE

Moshiach is Here

Jenna scowled at the hostile doorman as she left the building on West End Avenue and walked toward Broadway. Hey, you creep, she thought, I'm not a home-breaker: his wife's already left! This neighborhood was definitely not her scene. Why did Roger live up here, anyway? All these kids, baby strollers bumping you right and left, as though these mousy moms owned the street! Children crying everywhere, even in nice restaurants, like the boy last night: "I don't *want* any crème brûlée!" Then why not leave the kid home, with Oreos? Now if *she* had a child… but she didn't, and had no plans to have one, pregnant or not. Why compound Roger's hassles? The last thing he needed right now was another kid, along with his bitchy, alimony-grubbing, soon-to-be ex.

The garage on 87th disgorged a big black SUV, which zoomed so close it brushed her skirt; a little boy in the back seat stuck out his tongue at her. She stuck out hers back, and the father in his yarmulke turned and glowered at her over his shoulder, almost hitting a passing taxi. Serves you right, she thought: if you want to live in the city, why don't you walk? She smiled, remembering the time she'd yelled at an Orthodox Jew who'd elbowed her aside on the street: "Watch out, I'm a shiksa—on the rag!"

Well, she wasn't on the rag now, hadn't been for a couple of months. She even *felt* different already. Inflated, somehow, kinder and slower, more womanly, slightly bovine. Her small boobs were bigger, as Roger had noticed last night, although she hadn't told him anything yet. Which was what had given her the idea of buying a bra this morning: it wasn't going to last very long, so why not enjoy being zaftig for a bit? She looked at the ads in the windows of Victoria's Secret, then strode in, past the stony-faced large black guard, over to the drawers of 36 B's. She found a black lace bra and tried it on, admiring the way her fuller breasts suddenly blossomed into cleavage. It would be hard to give this up.

Out on the sidewalk again, she paused, wondering whether to go back to Roger's, or down to Zabar's to get something for lunch. Thinking of the disapproving doorman, she decided to head downtown. Past Origins and Coach and Harry's Shoes, Broadway turning into one big fat mall. She remembered Benny's, the little hamburger joint that used to be around here, up on the corner of 89th, that had hung on for so long, while Broadway around it fell prey to the conglomerates and condos. Eating there with Sebby, her first boyfriend after she'd come to the City. He was an actor, too, in "Fiddler" with her, her first job. Sebby was from Brooklyn and very funny: how he used to make her laugh with his lawyer jokes! What's the difference between a sperm and a lawyer? A sperm has one chance in a million of becoming a human being! Once she'd almost strangled laughing, on a bite of burger that had gone down the wrong way. Where was Sebby now? Still, it *was* nice to visit Roger on weekends up here in his spacious apartment, with its views of the Hudson and parquet floors. Her studio in the Village was so small...

In front of Zabar's, a dark young man with dreadlocks handed Jenna a small card that proclaimed **"Moshiach is Here!"** It showed a smiling old Jew with a black hat and white beard, who was proclaimed to be the Rebbe King Messiah. She idly turned it over and scanned the seven laws written on the back: "Believe in One G-d. Do not blaspheme. Do not murder (respect and value human life, including unborn babies)..." Oh, give me a fucking break, she thought, as she entered the store, which was, predictably, a mad house at ten on Sunday morning.

She made her way to the delicatessen, where an old lady and a yuppy guy were glaring at each other, apparently disputing the next ticket from the machine. A red-haired little boy stood beside an old man with side curls in a fur hat. She took a ticket, watching the kid as he stared up, open-mouthed, at the dazzling display of smoked fish and a bright tower of panettone on top of the counter.

"Vut you vaunt here?" the old man asked the child. "Here is nothing!"

Jenna laughed. The old man glared at her.

"Here is *everything*," she said.

The boy smiled, but his grandfather pulled him away, muttering about "the goyim."

She watched, longingly, as the boy was hauled along, still looking back at her. She might not be a bad mother, after all, she thought, staring at the card with the so-called King Messiah. Maybe next year, when she and Roger were more stable, and the divorce was over. But next year she would be thirty-eight, and her eggs would be that much staler, and who knew about Roger's sperm, at forty-five? Maybe, maybe, they should seize the day.

Jenna thought of the Off Broadway play she was in now, and how she couldn't possibly go on playing the sexy secretary for more than a couple of months, if the play ran that long. Easy to feign pregnancy, hard to hide it. Someone else could step in, though: Roger, as producer, could see to that.

"A pound of Nova," she said to the Hispanic girl behind the counter. "And pickles."

Originally published in *Our Stories*. © 2011

JUDITH BANNON SNOW

The 43rd Year Family Reunion

A MEMOIR

I was in a panic. I had secured a long-coveted position at Los Alamos National Laboratory in New Mexico. The job required obtaining a top secret security clearance, which in itself was not a problem. The problem was that the FBI agents who conducted the investigation were required to interview all current and former spouses—not boyfriends, not lovers, not cohabitants—just spouses. I didn't worry about my second husband, Dan, whom I had left three years earlier.

The problem was my first husband, Hunter, whom I had left abruptly and had neither seen nor spoken with in 26 years. I knew he needed to be forewarned, but I was terrified. Then I had an idea: I would ask our son, John, for help. I called him immediately.

"John, this is Mom. I need to get a security clearance and the FBI is going to interview Hunter. He needs to know this is going to happen. Will you call him?"

"No."

"No? You won't? Why not?"

"You should call him yourself."

"I can't. I haven't talked to him in 26 years. It would be horrible."

'No, Mom, it wouldn't. Hunter would love to hear from you. Really, he would. You need to call him."

There was no help for it. As I dialed the phone my terror increased.

"Hello?" It was Hunter.

"Hunter, this is Judith."

"What's wrong with your voice?"

"What?"

"Your voice. You sound so quavery."

"Well, I'm nervous."

"Why should you be nervous?"

I couldn't believe it, John was right. The same old Hunter. As if nothing had happened.

Thus began a long overdue healing process for Hunter and me.

My security clearance went through without a hitch.

Hunter and my relationship had begun at Whitman College. During our last two years there, we spent much of our time together in his cozy basement apartment. Ironically, it was a far better place to study than anywhere on campus. Hunter was a year behind me, so after graduation, I spent the next year at Reed College, 200 miles to the west, where I earned an M.A. in Teaching Chemistry.

After the year was over, Hunter and I married and had our son John. It was the first time we had actually lived together. Everything changed. Hunter, for reasons I had no way of understanding at the time, could do nothing to help with the household. I had a part-time job as an analytical chemist testing well water for the state of Washington. We had a division of labor: I did everything and Hunter did nothing. The only thing he could do, and did well, was talk. He was brilliant, articulate, charming, and funny. I was sinking under the weight of the responsibility I was shouldering and had lost hope for any positive future for my son and me. I felt desperate, afraid, and unmoored.

It was at this time I became romantically involved with Hunter's friend, Dan, who was attending the University of Washington. Dan, also married, said he wanted children, but his wife of three years did not. He not only seemed to become committed to me, but he also became very attached to my son

John. He seemed to be everything Hunter was not. Dan even changed John's diapers without being asked. Dan was able to take charge of any situation and master it. It was clear that he could successfully support a family. Although riddled with guilt, I saw this relationship as an escape from my dire predicament.

That evening Dan and I confronted our spouses, informed them of our decision to marry, and left abruptly with the intention of never seeing either one of them again. I took baby John and went to live with my mother. Dan rented a basement room nearby.

At first, I experienced tremendous relief. The dreary future I had foreseen for my son and me was averted. We would be part of a prosperous, stable family. John would have brothers and sisters. I would be the accomplished and vibrant stay-at-home mom I was meant to be. I even imagined that Dan would be a loving, supportive husband and father, just like my dad had been. I felt so fortunate—it felt too good to be true.

As we waited for our respective divorces to go through, I started to feel uncomfortable about my gradual loss of control in the relationship. Also, there was an almost imperceptible shift in our path forward. Most things that we talked of, dreamed about, and agreed upon never came to pass.

Then, shortly before our marriage, the promised honeymoon in San Francisco was scrapped. "We really can't afford it now. We'll go sometime later," he said.

On the day of our wedding, John, then almost two years old, was flushed and running a low grade fever.

"We need to cancel our Edgewater Hotel room for tonight. John is sick," he said.

"But we planned this as our honeymoon. He can stay here with my mother."

"We are not leaving John with anyone while he is sick," he replied angrily.

We spent our wedding night in my mother's bed. This 'honeymoon' foreshadowed the paucity of our future.

Dan finished his doctorate in psychology and secured a postdoctoral position at the Colorado Medical Center. We left Seattle for Denver as soon as possible, even though baby Kate was just eight days old. Dan wanted to put the shame and ruthlessness of our divorces behind us. His objective was to sever all connections with friends and classmates, and to never look back.

Dan especially wanted to minimize John's visitations with Hunter, who still lived in Seattle. He forbade me to see or talk to Hunter. His reason was always some version of "loving me so much" that it pained him to see me with another man, especially my former husband. What I didn't realize was that Dan was gradually taking control of my life. I was intoxicated by my infatuation with this "white knight" and with my amazing, undeserved romance. Although I at one level I could sense that I was succumbing to an illusion, it was so compelling that I was willing to forgo my independence and individuality to preserve it.

Dan was determined to raise John as his own firstborn. He was constantly testing John's IQ and developmental skills, getting upset when John couldn't identify a line drawing of a pitcher. Never mind that John had never seen a pitcher. At one point, Dan was convinced John was autistic. He even forced the left-handed child to use only his right

Although he tested Kate—could she hold a rattle correctly at seven weeks—Dan's main focus was on John. As my son grew older, he developed many of the characteristics, expressions, and mannerisms of Hunter, even though their interactions were rare. This drove Dan nuts.

Despite his outstanding performance during his two years in Denver, Dan was not offered a permanent job in Colorado. This was because his academic advisor had become aware of his unprofessional and inappropriate behavior with respect to the youth group he was leading. Dan applied for and was offered a professorship at the Yale School of Medicine. We left for Connecticut when son Adam was just two months old.

My relationship with Dan was falling apart because I found out he was being unfaithful. I was ready to call it quits, but he begged me to stay. He swore that everything was in the past and would never occur again. Despite his promises, I knew I could never be certain of his fidelity; I decided to develop a career of my own.

With Dan's encouragement, I began a doctoral program at Wesleyan University. I was the only woman in my physical chemistry group and the only grad student with children—when I started school, the children were two, four, and seven. I specialized in laser spectroscopy. It turned out that there was not much call in Connecticut for laser spectroscopists, but after I received my PhD, I was fortunate enough to secure a postdoctoral position in chemical physics at Yale, followed by an appointment there as research faculty in applied physics.

During this time family life was fraught with strife. Relentless fighting, yelling, and disrespect—nothing like the family I grew up in, and although I tried, there was nothing I could do to change it. The children managed to find their own friends in the neighborhood, but Dan and I did not. We did have "couple" friends that we frequently saw in New Haven, but I had no close friends of my own. Neither did Dan, which I realized was how he wanted it. We had a one-week vacation a year, but no other personal travel in the twenty years we were together. All work and no play certainly made for dull family living.

John was ten when we decided, on the strong advice of a child psychologist, to tell Kate and Adam that John had a different biological father. John begged us not to tell them, fearing rejection. As expected, the two younger kids, Kate and Adam, were extremely distraught—but within 30 minutes they were over it and everything was back to normal.

This did not become an issue until Dan and I finally separated for good, after he had another blatant affair. He wanted visitation rights with Kate and Adam, but not with John.

"I'm not going without John," said Kate.

"I'm not going either. It's all three of us or none of us," said Adam.

They were adamant and never relented.

Although they were grown, with only Adam living at home, Kate and John came back to live with me as well. It was wonderful, although sad at times—at lot like living in a dormitory with no curfew and no regulations.

It was at this time John told me that he had decided to become a journalist, despite having no experience whatsoever in the area.

"John, don't you think you should get some education in journalism first? You never worked on the school paper or even on the yearbook."

"No, I don't need more education," he said.

I was skeptical, thinking this surely was a dead-end strategy. John worked his way up from sports reporting in a local weekly, to municipal reporting in a daily, to having his own byline in the nationally known Hartford Courant.

"John, I am so proud of you."

"Mom, I am going to apply to the Medill School of Journalism at Northwestern."

Wow. No comment. He was accepted, earned a masters degree, and met his future wife, Lila.

Two years before Dan and I separated, I attended a laser conference in Seattle. On the last day, I was saying goodbye to my mother, who was leaving Seattle for her home on Vashon Island. Uncharacteristically, and wistfully, she looked at me and said, "I miss Hunter."

After my time at Yale, I worked for the Department of the Navy for eight years as a civilian physicist. I led the marine optics group in the Navy's submarine research lab in New London. I had good friends in the area, Mimi and Greg.

Three weeks after I had decided my relationship with Dan

was over for good, I invited Mimi for lunch. She said, "Why don't you come for dinner instead? Greg has a old roommate who is visiting."

"Is he married?" I kidded.

"No, but he's not your type."

That's when I met Richard Kramer, who absolutely was my type, and I his.

For a year and a half we had a long distance relationship, me in Connecticut and he in Taos, New Mexico. It was a relatively happy and calm time in my life; I had escaped a dysfunctional marriage of twenty years, and developed a positive and loving relationship with Richard. My children had escaped a dysfunctional family situation and were beginning to get settled.

In a great stroke of luck, my Navy lab sponsored me in a one-year program as a Sloan Fellow at Stanford's Graduate School of Business to earn an M.S. in Management. That year at Stanford was first time I lived with Richard, who moved to be near me for the duration. He made me cappuccino every morning, dinner every night, and audited classes during the day. We decided we wanted to live together permanently, preferably in New Mexico.

That is when I applied for and got a position at Los Alamos National Laboratory. After my scare regarding contacting Hunter about my security clearance investigation, everything went smoothly. Richard and I moved into a charming old adobe house in the Rio Grande River Valley.

After a few months, we decided to marry. We had a lovely ceremony at the Lighthouse Inn in New London, Connecticut, with about 40 guests. I wore a flowing ivory silk tunic and tea-length skirt, with a crown of small flowers in my hair. Kate was my maid of honor. John and Adam were the groomsmen. It was a glorious September day and after the reception dinner, the entire wedding party took the short walk from the Inn down to Long Island Sound. Richard and I honeymooned in Maine for a week, and then returned to our home in New Mexico.

After my first phone call warning Hunter about the FBI

investigation for my Los Alamos security clearance, we had been in contact frequently. On our next trip to Seattle to see family and friends Richard and I decided to meet Hunter and his girlfriend, Nan. We met at an unassuming Thai restaurant in West Seattle. At first it was awkward—I hadn't seen Hunter in over 20 years. We ended up hitting it off famously and the four of us thoroughly enjoyed our time together.

Not long after our Seattle visit, I spotted a large creamy envelope in the mail. It was a wedding invitation from Hunter and Nancy.

"Richard, what do you think?"

"Why not? Let's go."

Their outdoor wedding at Point Defiance in Tacoma was delightful. The weather was perfect; John and Nancy were on cloud nine.

After that, Richard and I saw Hunter and Nancy periodically. They visited us in New Mexico and we often stayed with them when we visited Seattle. Although John saw Hunter and Nancy often, he was never around when we four "parents" had these visits together. John had no idea of how often the four of us got together, and how strong our friendship had become.

On another of our visits to Seattle, Hunter got up from the couch and said, "I'm going to clean out the cats' litter box."

"What?" I thought, "Hunter offering to take care of anything, especially such an unpleasant job?"

I was shocked to learn that Hunter had had undiagnosed clinical depression and off-the-charts ADHD, both of which were being successfully treated with appropriate meds. It was then I understood the tragedy of our brief, unsuccessful marriage. It wasn't that Hunter *wouldn't* help—it was that he *couldn't* help. Because of his undiagnosed and debilitating condition, he was unable to perform straightforward tasks that were taken for granted by the rest of us.

Not long after John and Lila earned graduate degrees in journalism, John became a senior editor for a hunting and fishing magazine based in Manhattan. After several years of commuting from suburban Norwalk, Connecticut to the city, he convinced the magazine's management to let him move to Montana, since most of his work was outdoors.

The Thursday before John was going to leave for Montana, Richard and I—who were then retired and living in New Haven—went down to Norwalk to say goodbye. John was driving the Jeep out to Bozeman find a house to rent and get settled. Four weeks later, Lila and the two kids would drive out in the minivan.

Lila looked at me and said, "Why don't you drive out with John? I don't like the idea of his driving alone."

"Yeah, Mom, come with me."

I looked at Richard, who nodded.

"When are you leaving?" I asked.

"Saturday or Sunday."

Although I had three-quarters of my margarita remaining and was still in full control of my senses, I agreed.

"Mom, let's book your one-way return ticket from Montana now. The computer is in the other room."

Within fifteen minutes, everything was arranged.

At noon on Sunday, we set out in John's seldom-used Jeep Cherokee, towing a 19-foot outboard fishing boat. Within four hours, the Jeep was choking and sputtering. Fortunately, we were within sight of a T/A Truck Stop. As we rolled into the parking area, the Jeep jerked to a halt. We arranged to get it serviced the following day and, with no motels in sight, managed to get the last available room at the truck stop.

As we entered the room, John said, "It smells." These words came from the man who several months every year "sleeps rough" in everything from subzero temperatures in the Arctic to sweltering heat in the Amazon. On the other hand, perhaps either would be preferable to the pervasive odor of mildew.

"There is only one bed," he wailed.

"This is true."

"We are going to have to sleep in the same bed," he said.

"We are," I said.

"We haven't slept in the same bed since I was a baby."

We survived the night.

This was the first of several breakdowns during the trip. We suffered through August in the Midwest without the benefit of the Jeep's air conditioning, which had stopped working on the second day. Despite the heat and discomfort, our mother/son trip was a great success.

We had a lovely dinner beside the Mississippi River in La Crosse, Wisconsin. South Dakota offered three special treats: looping through Badlands National Park (purple, yellow, orange and red buttes, pinnacles, and spires); transit through the Harley-Davidson Motorcycle Rally in Sturgis (wild and crazy); and the world's only Corn Palace in Mitchell (a Moorish Revival structure totally covered in corn cobs, nailed on fresh every year).

We had a great BBQ dinner with a colleague of John's in Sheridan, Wyoming. Our last stop was a visit to Custer's Last Stand at the Little Big Horn Battlefield Monument in Montana.

When we arrived at our destination in Bozeman, John was treated like a rock star almost everywhere we went—the bank, the accountant, the car dealer, the fishing and hunting store, and so on.

Often I got the impassioned query, "You're John Snow's mother?"

"Well," I thought, "yes I am."

John and I were invited to stay at the home of John's real estate agent, Sara. On a previous trip, John and Lila had hired her to represent them. She had been particularly taken with Lila.

Sara and her boyfriend, Doug, lived in a spacious home, beautifully situated on a hillside overlooking the valley and the mountains beyond. The house had two suites: a master suite at one end and a two-bedroom suite with private bath connected by a large sitting room at the other. The large kitchen, living room, and balcony separated the two ends of the home.

Sara and Doug had planned an extended fishing vacation. As I was to find out after extensive questioning, absolutely everyone in Bozeman fished, usually every day. The only people I could find who didn't fish were a couple that danced the two-step most evenings at the Mint Café and Bar in Belgrade.

Hunter was scheduled to come out to Bozeman when Sara and Doug were away, and they offered him the master bedroom suite. John, Hunter, and I enjoyed a relaxing time in the luxurious home with its balconies and outdoor spaces. The weather was very fine and there was rarely a bug to be seen. Walking and hiking around the hilly neighborhood, we admired the impressive homes with their beautifully landscaped grounds and gardens. We created delicious meals in the well-appointed kitchen, ate our dinners on the balcony, and watched the spectacular Montana sunsets.

Sara was a neat freak, so we decided to make certain we left the house in mint condition. Thus the day before she and Doug returned, the three of us set about cleaning the place. Hunter, who when we were married was incapable of doing anything, took to cleaning with a vengeance. He moved all the furniture to vacuum the carpets beneath. He and I changed the sheets in the master bedroom, Hunter doing perfect hospital corners on the top. "Where did he learn that?" I thought.

"I feel like a hotel maid," said Hunter.

"Me too."

When we were finished, the three of us moved to the balcony to share a bottle of Sara's favorite wine, La Crema Chardonnay.

John was standing between Hunter and me. He looked at each of us and said, "I feel like I am in a reality show—The 43rd Family Reunion."

JENNIFER J. FRANCHERE

Wishing for Forever

"**M**ommy, I'm scared my wish won't come true." My eight-year-old daughter looked up at me from our bedtime snuggle.

"Why? Do you want to tell me what it is?"

"I can't, because then it won't be true."

"If I guessed at what your wish is, and you just nod yes or shake your head no, then you aren't really telling me. What do you think, does that work?"

"Yes, I think so."

"Is your wish about me?"

"Yes, and Dad too. And I could add my sister."

"Is it that we always stay healthy?"

"Kind of."

"Is it that we always stay together?"

"Yes, but it's more than that. Always always."

"Oh, that your dad and I would live forever?"

"Mm hm," she nodded and curled tighter into me.

She has brought this up more than this once. Last week, she asked me why people can't live forever. I laughed it off saying the world would be pretty crowded if no one ever left it. She thought that it would be fine as long as people stopped having babies.

"But, then that would be sad," I responded.

We would do anything, give anything to our children. But this, we cannot give, cannot promise. Words might find their way out to reassure, to comfort, yet in the end are just words.

Our children seem to sense that from an early age.

In our bedtime conversation, I asked the same of her, "Promise me that *you'll* live forever, because I don't want to ever know a world without you in it."

She grew quiet and did not answer.

The next day, I learned that around the same time we were snuggling and talking, a father of one of her classmates was dying. I didn't even have a whole day to keep up the illusion for my daughter that maybe we *could* live forever, because by then I then had to tell her about her friend's father.

She responded surprisingly lightly. I had worried overmuch, I guess. Or maybe it was an easy way for her to deal with the news.

After the girls went to bed, I sought the very same reassurances from my husband, "Don't you ever leave me like that."

"I'll try. You do the same."

When you marry, you think only of the time you will spend with your husband or wife. It hardly occurs to you to think of the time you will face without him or her. Yet it is most likely, and inevitable, that it will happen. Julian Barnes's words stay with me: "Every love story is a potential grief story."

As I see it happen to people I know, I imagine how they must suffer with having to re-imagine all they thought their future would be, now without their partner.

How is my daughter's friend, this intelligent, funny, bright nine-year-old girl, going to grow up without her father in her life? He will not be with her at the important milestones of her life, starting next month with the father-daughter dance.

I want to keep all of the partings at bay, but know I am ultimately powerless to do so. Every sudden loss of a friend or acquaintance reminds me of that. *I* need that reassuring snuggle in the night too, to tell me that we will all really live forever, and not to ever worry about a time that we will be apart. I wish it could be true.

The Haddam Writers Group

Judith M. Cooke enjoys writing about quirky characters, is a full-time pastor in the United Church of Christ, and has an unhealthy relationship with caffeine.

Jennifer J. Franchere volunteers far more often than she should for school, scouts, church, and non-profits. Married to a serial runner, she parents two daughters and a greyhound.

Michael J. Gordon is a retired urban planner, professor, businessman, and ad executive who is finally doing what he always wanted: to write, and is having the time of his life.

Kent Jarrell is a former Washington-based journalist and crisis management consultant who has retired to a refuge on the banks of the Connecticut River to watch the tidal flow.

James E. McKie, Jr. spent three decades as a biophysical research scientist. His writing is mostly creative non-fiction, based on memory, journals, letters, and historical research.

Paula Spurlin Paige is an Adjunct Professor, Emerita of Italian and French at Wesleyan University. Recent stories have been published in Reed Magazine and Newfound.

Isabelle D. Seggerman had a long career in the world of Art and Antiques. As the wife of a wine importer, she traveled extensively. She has been published over the past 35 years.

Judith Bannon Snow spent a life in science: spectroscopy, nonlinear optics, underwater laser communications, and executive management. She writes, paints, and coaches.

Rae Studholme heeded the siren call of Lake Pocotopaug and returned to Connecticut from Colorado. She's been a teacher, social worker, journalist, wife, mother, and writer.